Educating Kenilw

CW00518997

Educating Kenilworth

Leonard Unsworth

YOUCAXTON PUBLICATIONS

OXFORD & SHREWSBURY

Contents

List of Pictures

1. Churchill visiting Coventry Cathedral.
   http://commons.wikimedia.org/wiki/
   File:Winston_Churchill_at_Coventry_Cathedral_
   cph.3a18421.
2. Saint Nicholas Church Kenilworth.
3. Parochial Church Hall Kenilworth.
4. School Gate.
5. Alice and Francis Lenny's Grandparents.
6. Beatrice and Reuben, Lenny's Grandparents.
7. Lenny's Dad.
8. Dream Machine. Three Wheel Box Van.
   http://commons.wikimedia.org/wiki/
   File:Raleigh_Karryall_3_Wheel_Van_1935_-_Flickr_-_
   mick_-_Lumix.
9. Blackie, Jean, Lenny.
10. Notingate. Jean, Lenny.
11. Vauxhall Velox.http://commons.wikimedia.org/wiki/
    File:Vauxhall_Velox_ca_1953_in_Hertfordshire.jpg
12. Kenilworth War Memorial.
13. Choir Team on Parliament Piece, Lenny Front Row.
14. Gordon Jones. Middlesbrough Captain.
15. World Cup Willie, 1966.
    http://commons.wikimedia.org/wiki/File:National_
    Football_Museum_Manchester_5697_(14180312576).jpg

Preface

The past never really leaves us. Lenny assumed that he had moved on from his often difficult adolescence years half a century ago. Then the chance discovery of some old photographs brought it all back. He realised that the things that happen to us in our formative years never really leave us; that the way a young boy or girl is treated by people in positions of authority can set them on a particular track that has a great impact on how their life unfolds. Since that day, he has spent much of his time thinking about those early years and a chain of events that set him on course towards a future that could have been very different. This is much more than just another childhood memoir; it is also a deeply personal exploration of one child's experience.

Lenny was an ordinary child in most respects. He was from a respectable home; his dad had a skilled job in the engineering industry with an important role to play during the Second World War, and his mum worked part time and took care of the children. The family lived in the attractive small town of Kenilworth, a few miles away from Coventry in the Midlands. Coventry had been absolutely devastated in the war, which ended a few years before Len's birth, and Kenilworth had not been spared either. Len and his childhood friends grew up playing on the rubble of the Globe Hotel that had been bombed, killing evacuees who had been staying there in the expectation that they would avoid the blitz.

The 1950s and 60s was a time of social upheaval everywhere in Britain. Conventions were being flouted and the culture was in a state of transition. The Empire was in its last throes as one after another of its former colonies claimed independence. There was a growing understanding that it was time to start doing things differently. In this context, the education system was overhauled with a view to creating the sort of society that a modern Britain would need. 'Educating Kenilworth,' meant that a brand-new school, intended to exemplify this shiny modernity, was required for the town's girls and boys, among them a thirteen-year-old Lenny. Heading the new school was a woman who was already an established headmistress, having led a well-known girls' school in nearby Coventry for years. As he was good at sports, and confident with girls, at first everything went well. But Lenny struggled with authority and frequently found himself at odds with the headmistress, who seemed to have no idea how to deal with boys. She seemed to be trying to replicate the girls' school she had led so successfully – but this was a mixed school and, even more importantly, the social norms in Britain as a whole were changing rapidly. Kenilworth's brave new attempt to provide an innovative and daring modern education for its youth wasn't working out – not for Lenny, and not for any of the other boys who didn't fit the mould the headmistress was used to.

Things culminated when, on a school trip, Lenny was accused of stealing a camera. In fact, he had simply found a lost camera and used it to shoot a number of images of his classmates. He was stripped of his role of head boy and informed that he was now attending the school on sufferance, and would be expected to leave as soon he turned the legal age of departure at fifteen.

Cycling away from the school for the last time, his sight blurred by the tears streaming down his face, Lenny was prematurely launched on his journey throughout adulthood.

That First Day

Memory is a funny thing. Events can apparently disappear from mind, only to be brought back years later by a familiar smell, a few bars of an old tune, or the fading images of happy days from long before.

A few years ago my younger sister, Julie, was celebrating her fiftieth birthday and she had rooted out a selection of old photographs for the occasion, with the idea of decorating the party room with images from our shared past. It was all so long ago it was fascinating looking at those faded images of ourselves as youngsters and of Mum and Dad before they grew old and frail. The black and white images showed us as ghosts from a past that is gone in one way, but that will always live within us in another.

'What's this then?' I said, reaching for a box. 'I don't think I've seen these ones.'

'Oh,' Julie said, 'it's just a bunch of old photos I took down from the house. They must have been stuffed in a box when Dad was still alive. Goodness knows what they're all about. Have a look and see if there's anything good in there.'

Inside the box mingled with some family snaps was a bunch of black and white photographs that I had taken when I was just fifteen years old, on a school trip to Wales. I remembered taking the images, but didn't know that the film had been developed. Dad must have had it done years before and then put the photographs away. There they had rested for all these years, just waiting for me to look at them for the first time.

I hadn't realised it that day, wouldn't for several weeks, but taking those images had been a pivotal moment in my life; one that would go on to shape the future.

Gradually as weeks went by I was transported back to the past, back to a time long before I even knew what sort of adult life I was going to live, and back even before the school trip, to the very start of my journey through the education system; a journey that would end abruptly when I was just fifteen years old…

§

My father grew up in Coventry, and my mother in Darlington, which is far away in the north-east. Dad had worked as an aircraft technician during the Second World War and was involved in the recovery of damaged aeroplanes. It was a very important job that took him all over the country (unlike most people he ran a car during the war, because he needed to be able to travel from one aerodrome to another at a moments notice). On one of his trips, this time to the airbase at Catterick, he met Mum and they fell in love and decided to get married and start a family, despite the fact that they had very different personalities. Before her marriage, Mum had worked on the railway. It was a traditionally male job, but so many young men were away at war that a lot of the positions that they had once held now went to girls and women. After the war, many of those women were expected to give up their jobs for the returning men, and to go back to the kitchen. Most of them did, but it was difficult to relinquish the new freedom and independence that working

Picture 1: Churchill Visiting Coventry Cathedral.

in these non-traditional roles had brought them. Mum never talked about it to me, but no doubt she found it hard too; that might help to explain some of the melancholy and dissatisfaction that so often characterised her adult life.

As well as giving up her job, Mum left her home, her parents and family, to settle in Kenilworth, near Dad's home town of Coventry. It was all very different to what she was used to; the landscape and accent were different, and the area had been much more badly affected by the war. Coventry was famously nearly destroyed and even outlying towns like Kenilworth had been bombed. Starting a new life amid the rubble and trauma that were the aftermath of the war must have been a big challenge for the lass from the north.

§

I can still remember my very first day at school, when I was aged four and a half. It's such a wrench, being torn away from Mum and the kitchen and everything that feels safe and familiar, that I expect most people can remember their own first day at school, and went through many of the same emotions. For me, it was a traumatic affair. I must have been nervous beforehand – despite the fact that my older sister, Jean, had already been in school for two years – because Mum tried to reassure me, saying that if I didn't like it, I wouldn't have to stay. I took her at her word, and rather assumed that I wouldn't like it, and that I would soon be coming back home again. Of course, Mum was lying, trying to make her life that little bit easier as she hauled her unwilling son to school. Despite my attempts to drag my feet and delay the proceedings, we eventually reached the school playground, where she handed me over to my new teacher.

'Goodbye now, Lenny, love,' she said brightly. 'I'll see you later!'

Mum turned on her heel and walked briskly out the gate, undoubtedly enjoying the prospect of spending several hours with no children tugging at her and demanding attention. I watched her retreating back with absolute horror as she got further away.

'*No*, Mum,' I screamed. 'Don't leave me. I'm coming with you! I don't like it here; you said I wouldn't have to stay!'

As fast as I could, I raced to the gate, my heart pounding in absolute panic, and tears streaming down my face, my eyes fixed on Mum as she walked away. She hesitated, turned and looked back. Was I going to get a reprieve after all? My heart leapt in hope and anticipation and for a moment I thought that it was all going to be OK.

But the school was used to this sort of thing and one of the members of staff caught me at the gate and returned me unceremoniously to the teacher.

'Just go,' the teacher called over to Mum. 'He'll be fine. We can handle it. It'll be easier for everyone when you've left.'

Sniffling with defeat, and absolutely devastated about the fact that Mum had revealed herself to be the sort of person who couldn't be trusted. I accompanied the teacher to the classroom, which was filled with kids in similar states of shock and dismay. We took no comfort in numbers. I suspect that each of us was going through the same spectrum of emotions, from rage at being duped to terror that our mums might just leave us there and never come back at all.

I don't remember what happened next, but later that day I had calmed down enough to play with the wooden building blocks the teacher provided. I clearly remember piling them up, one on top of the other, to create a tower. I looked proudly at my edifice.

'Well now,' I thought. 'This ain't too bad after all!'

If only school had really been all about playing with blocks!

Apart from that first day I have just a few rather muddled memories of my first year or so at school. I don't even remember

Picture 2: Saint Nicholas Church Kenilworth.

the name of the teacher. But I believe I settled in reasonably quickly, like all the other kids. I'm sure that most of us started out bawling.

§

The school's biggest logistical obstacle was feeding everyone. This meant getting over one hundred kids from School Lane half a mile away and back to the tables each dinner time, whether it was raining, hailing or snowing. The teachers lined us all up in twos and marched the column of kids through an avenue of lime trees making a meandering path, never was there a more beautiful sight which on special occasions can still be seen to this day, then passed the ruins of Saint Mary's Abbey in the grounds of Saint Nicholas' Church to the Parochial

Picture 3: Parochial Church Hall Kenilworth.

Church Hall where dinner was served. The hall also had rooms above that doubled as extra class rooms for our school when needed, and there was a boys' club at the rear. For many years to come, traipsing over to the Church Hall for lunch would be our daily routine.

In the 1950s, when I was in St Nicholas C of E Primary School, polio was still an absolute scourge and the terror of all young families. For reasons that weren't entirely clear, polio had gone from being a relatively rare disease to one that emerged in the form of an epidemic in the late nineteenth century, killing large numbers of children and leaving others paralysed. Right up until the late fifties and early sixties, when a vaccine became widely available, waves of polio would crash over communities, leaving behind children who were paralysed or otherwise impaired and, in the worst cases, bereaved parents.

From an early age we were told awful stories about children being placed inside an iron lung to help them breath, but in reality for seventy percent of kids they were being placed inside an iron coffin. We were warned to do everything we could to avoid becoming ill. When there was an outbreak in our school, closing it for several weeks, everyone was aghast. Most of it went over my head at the time, and even now, a dad myself I can only imagine how terrified the parents must have been. Polio is caused by a virus, and there was a degree of under-standing of how it could be transmitted from one child to another. In consequence, we were each given a little towel and a bar of carbolic soap of our own, as well as a special scrubbing brush that we were instructed to use on our hands and nails at every available opportunity.

The danger of the situation was brought home when, about two years after I started school, a child died, a little boy called Peter Soden who had been in my sister's class, and when a couple of other children were left with paralysis as a result of the disease. For us kids, however, we seemed invincible, and washing and scrubbing our hands constantly struck us as an appalling waste of time when we could have been outside in the playground having a great time. Periodically we lapsed from the onerous hygiene regime. One day I got caught for not washing my hands, or not washing them properly, and I was in serious trouble.

'Right,' said the teacher, 'that's it; down to the head with you! We can't have you not washing your hands properly.'

With great trepidation I made my way to the principals office, where harsh words were spoken to me at some length. Just when I thought that it was over, I was told to extend my hand.

'What for?' I asked.

'So you don't forget to wash your hands again, I'm going to give you something you'll remember,' the Headmaster Mr Jones said.

Well, I know what that meant – and I also knew that I had no choice but to get it over with. Already wincing, I held out my hand and received the three great stinging slaps with the cane.

Today I would be absolutely furious if anybody lifted a hand on one of my children, and have been assured personally by the Head-Teacher Mrs Mohacsi, that now in St. Nicholas Primary, (one of the finest schools in England) there is no hitting of children whatsoever. But in my day corporal punishment was par for the course. If you went home and complained to your parents that you'd been caned, the usual response was, 'Well, what did you do to deserve it?' – And given the level of panic about polio at that time, I doubt that I would have received much sympathy from Mum and Dad. I'd got what I deserved.

After the caning I returned to the classroom, pressing my aching hand against the side of my leg until it stopped hurting so much. My friends looked at me with a mixture of sympathy and voyeurism and I told them how much the caning had hurt, not leaving out any details. I never did forget to wash my hands properly after that, so it must have worked.

Perhaps because fewer diseases could be successfully treated then, the medical profession seemed to be almost excessively keen on chopping bits off or out of any child who seemed to be prone to infection. I can't tell you how many kids in my class had their tonsils out, but it was a very common operation in those days. At the time, the prevailing medical belief was that tonsils served no function at all, although nowadays we know that they are the body's first line of defence against disease. Anybody who suffered from a recurrent sore throat was packed off to the local hospital to have their tonsils removed. I was one of those unfortunates.

I can still remember the day I was taken to see Doctor Harger and him dictating my details into a Dictaphone I was only five, and the prospect of going to hospital terrified me, but the idea in those days was that kids should have a stiff upper lip and just deal with things like little soldiers. Parents tended not to be particularly sympathetic in the face of anxiety, perhaps partly because they had all lived through the war and knew very well what real stress felt like.

Dad brought me to Leamington Warneford hospital and handed me over to the matron. We said goodbye outside the ward; parents were not encouraged to come in or to comfort their children any more than strictly necessary; that would have looked like molly-coddling and the matron would have taken a dim view of that!

After the operation I was put to bed in a children's ward. Most of the beds contained other kids who had also had their tonsils removed – probably unnecessarily. I remember lying in the dark,

Picture 4: School Gate.

wishing I was home and watching the matron, who sat at a desk dimly illuminated with an angle-poise lamp. I felt very alone.

Not long after the tonsillectomy, I managed to injure myself quite badly in the playground. We were just mucking around. At some stage I curled my hand around the post of the school gate, and the next thing I knew the gate had slammed shut on one of my fingers, lopping the top of it right off. I can still remember as if it was yesterday how I felt as I tore up the yard screaming for help, with blood pouring out of me in an apparently endless torrent. I can recall the exact contours of the playground as I ran across; when I close my eyes I can return to the scene. It was back to the Warneford hospital for me, this time to have my finger dressed. A school photograph taken shortly afterwards shows me with my bandaged finger at a jaunty angle – and I don't look otherwise any the worse for wear!

Picture 5: Alice and Francis. Lenny's Grandparents.

At school, all the boys played the classic rough-and-tumble sports and games. I remember one of my friends called Steve playing conkers with another lad. One of the conkers broke and hit him in the eye and, in a state of pain and confusion, he ran into the school screaming, 'I'm blinded! I'm blinded!' after wearing an eye patch for a couple of days, he be alright!

Coventry's new cathedral was nearing completion and we were all invited to contribute one florin towards a stained glass window to help replace the ones that had mysteriously disappeared. Two bob was quite a *bit* in those days and would buy you a full portion of cod and chips.

By the time I was seven or eight, it had become evident that my talents lay in the area of sports. I loved all physical activity, and would have been perfectly happy if school had consisted entirely of sprinting up and down the playground. I was the fastest child in my age group and won the red ribbon for the hundred yards dash in the school sports day, which was held in Abbey Fields. That was one of the proudest moments of my young life. A great love of sport was something I had in common with various male family members. Dad was quite a silent man, not much of a talker, but he had told me stories of playing football, boxing and shooting in his younger days.

My Granddad, Mum's father, who had served in the First World War as a very young man, had played football for the army. On his visits to us, he used to lift up his shirt and show me the four marks on his body – two for the entry wounds where the bullets had gone in and two where they had gone out. He had also survived a gas attack, and told me all about it. In my child's mind, his stories of battleground heroism and playing football for the army were conflated. I just knew that I wanted to be like him and that I could start by playing football.

Then there was my cousin Gordon who was about five years older than me and already, as a schoolboy, being talked about as a serious contender for one of the big football clubs, but the headlines of the day were exemplified when I went into the back room at home to find my mum crying she had just been listening to the news, I said 'what's wrong Mum' she replied 'all those young boy's are dead.' She was referring to the Busby Babes and the Munich air disaster.

Mum and Dad were good parents in many ways, but they were rather distant, and I don't remember feeling that I could go to them with any little problems I was having. By the time I was seven or eight I had realised that the other kids in the class were all doing much better at reading than me. They seemed to be racing ahead while I still found picking out the words painfully difficult. I remember staring at the page and seeing the black letters all dancing about against the white background as though they were animated. The teacher, Mrs Jordan, knew that I was struggling with reading, but nothing much was ever done about it and I don't remember ever being taken aside and asked if I had any ideas about what might help. I don't know if my parents were made aware of the problem or if they thought it was a big deal or not. Maybe they just assumed that my strengths lay elsewhere and that it didn't really matter. I remember being graded at the end of one year and finding out that I'd come forty-third out of the class total of forty-five. I was rather despondent about this, and Dad tried to cheer me up: 'Never mind, son,' he said. 'There's still two behind you.'

The principal teacher of the school Mr Bentley was licensed to cane. He only had one eye which seamed to effect his accuracy when swiping down, either catching the edge of your wrist or finger ends, with his short stubby cane, in contrast to the long floppy one preferred by the Headmaster.

My failings at school bled into everyday life and I became quite nervous of anyone in a position of authority. One day I was taken from school to go to the dentist. Terrified, I ran away and hid in the Common. Mum wasn't able to keep up with me in the stiletto shoes that most women wore in those days. I can still hear her calling, 'Come back Len come back!' I just snuggled more tightly into my hiding place and didn't deign to answer. Eventually she left. I arrived home on my own at around five and was sent straight to bed by a very irate Dad.

My own approach to my academic short-fallings was to figure out ways to hide my difficulties as much as possible. I developed an excellent memory, along with an eye for detail, and was very good at reciting poetry, which may have given the impression that I was also able to read it with ease, although that was far from the case. I memorised *The Charge of the Light Brigade* and even won a class prize for being able to stand up in front of the headmaster and recite it. In fact, I won a prize for reciting poetry every year in primary school, and was always first.

I was very good at handicrafts, which offered me another chance to shine among my peers at school. There were forty-five children in my class and I was by far the best at making things. Handicrafts were taught by a different teacher to our usual form room one. At the end of one year, she brought all our work into the form room and asked Mrs Jordan, our usual teacher, who she thought had made the very best piece. She guessed a few names, and got it wrong each time, finally asking the winning pupil to raise their hand. I can still remember her air of disbelief when it was me! That was a very proud moment in my young life.

I had a box of Meccano which had given me the bug for mechanics and anything to do with machines and gadgets. I taught myself how to take bicycles apart and put them back together again with different size wheels and various handlebars and bells. While Dad didn't usually help, he did give me space in the garage to mess around in, and free access to the tool boxes and vice. The garage was a sectional one with an asbestos roof a sort of fore-runner of the flat-pack idea of today, and Dad had put it together himself. Asbestos turned out to be the single greatest cause of work related deaths in the United Kingdom, to this day.

My friendships in those days of primary school were the normal, uncomplicated friendships of childhood. I had a couple of great pals, one of whom was called Richard Snelson and lived in a little house called Quail's Cottage on farmland behind Kenilworth Castle. Richard had a great birds' egg collection. We used to sneak into the castle via a secret tunnel, taking a bottle of water with us. It was the height of fun going up to the dungeon and dropping the bottle so that we could watch the impact when it fell. My other friend was John Flowers, with whom I would play in the Common. On one fantastic occasion John's parents brought us both to Alton Towers in their brand-new Mini Minor. We all piled into the tiny car and made our way excitedly to Alton Towers for one of the best days of my early life.

Usually, John and I contented ourselves with a little snooker table that was mine but kept in his room. Whenever I went to his house we played snooker in his bedroom. It was all quite exotic for me, because my parents were much more reserved than John's and my sister and I were not allowed to bring friends up to our rooms. In fact, we weren't really encouraged to have friends over at all. For Mum and Dad, our family house was a private sanctuary from their busy lives and they slightly resented any intrusion into their space. That might sound a little harsh, but this attitude was still very common in the 1950s and 60s. People were simply much more private about their personal and family lives than they are today. Mum was also quite house-proud and I think that this also contributed to her reluctance to open the house to all and sundry.

I'll never forget the huge effort Mum put into spring cleaning every year, as though spring meant that the Queen herself might come and visit. All the pelmets were taken down and the curtains washed, dried and ironed before being put up again. Every item of furniture was cleaned, and every square inch of floor was scrubbed. Mum also worked at night in a hotel up the road, the King's Arms and Castle (locally famous for having briefly housed Sir Walter Scott, who was inspired by his stay to write the novel *Kenilworth*), which had a bar called The Vaults; it was a quiet, respectable venue and there was never any trouble with people getting drunk and into fights or anything like that, but she still worked late nights. I remember being allowed to stay up late during the school holidays and going around to the pub with Dad to collect her.

Kenilworth was a safe environment for the children growing up there. The town was small enough that parents felt confident about allowing their kids to play outside with only a minimum of supervision. There was lots of green space to run about on and, even more excitingly, the rubble from where the town had been bombed during the war was still very much in evidence. One of the worst things to happen in Kenilworth during the war years was the Globe Hotel being hit by a land mine. It had housed evacuees from the blitz who believed that they would be safe far away from the city and the heavy bombing. For us kids, growing up in the shadow of the war, it was simply an adventure playground with the prospect of finding the silver sword rumoured to be hidden on the site and we couldn't be dissuaded from clambering around on the remains of the buildings where so many people had died just a few years before.

Overall, Jean and I had quite a happy, if rather uneventful, childhood. We were unaware of the fact that Mum and Dad were having problems in their marriage, or at least I was. The lives of grown-ups seemed almost completely irrelevant to me. All I cared about was having fun, playing with my mates, football and fishing. Looking back now, I can see that Mum and Dad were very different, and that their contrasting approaches to life must often have been stressful for them both. Mum was quite vivacious. She liked to go out and meet people and have a nice time. Dad, instead, was sedate, even dour at times, and was extremely careful with money. His priorities in life were paying the bills and the mortgage and putting a little aside for a rainy day. He rarely let his hair down. Mum was also far from home and I think she missed her family and friends back in Darlington. In those days people didn't travel nearly as much as they do today and we rarely saw our grandparents. They came to visit at Easter, amid great excitement, and only very occasionally during the summer, but that was it.

One day, when I got home from school I found a note on the table. It wasn't addressed to anybody in particular so I picked it up and puzzled over it until I had figured out what it said. It was from Mum. She'd had enough, she said, and she had decided to leave home and return to Darlington, where she would stay with her parents. Dad would have to take care of my sister Jean and me on his own.

As the reality of the situation dawned on me, I burst into violent tears. How could Mum have left us? What would we do without her? Would we ever see her again?

That was the moment when the innocence of childhood left me and the beginning of a time of life in which I became increasingly oppositional towards the adults around me, while continuing to pursue success and admiration in the world of sports.

Picture 6: Beatrice and Reuben. Lennys Grandparents.

Life without Mum

Without his wife on the scene, Lenny's father had to care for Lenny and Jean on his own, and also hold down his job. It wasn't easy, and it was made more difficult by the fact that, in those days, fathers simply didn't know that much about child-care. With the whole family reeling at the shock of Mum's departure, Lenny's difficulty with reading and writing was largely overlooked and the only help he got was to be put out of the classroom to do lines. He had also become adept at concealing his problems in this area, and had established himself as a class joker – but because he was doing well at sports somehow his academic troubles were never really addressed.

At home he sought comfort in the familiar world of cogs and wheels and spent as much time as he could in the garage, working on his mechanical projects. Without Mum around he was having to do more things for himself and learned how to cook his favourite meal of double egg and chips. It wasn't easy. When he developed a cyst on his eye and had to go to hospital, Lenny went on his own, catching the bus in each direction.

The 11-plus exam was standard in the 1950s and 60s. Originally, it had been conceived of as a way to help teachers to figure out which sort of secondary school was suited to each child. In practice, it had become a system to weed out middle-class children and send them to grammar schools while everyone else was crammed into a secondary modern for a more

Picture 7: Lennys Dad.

'vocational' education that often overlooked, or ignored, individual students' academic difficulties. The occasional bright working class child made it through but they were the exception rather than the rule. Lenny's sister, Jean was a bright child and was devastated when she didn't quite pass and would not be going up to grammar school. Jean was positioned 12th in her class and the top 25 all went to grammar school apart from Jean who was excluded. The kids in Jeans class were quizzed as to which newspaper their dad read. They often wondered if Dad reading the wrong newspaper had anything to do with it or the family ethos. Lenny knew that he didn't stand a chance.

Without Mum on the scene Lenny's Grandmother who was then in her mid-eighties stepped in to help. She had raised eight children of her own, one of whom (also called Lenny) had died in childhood. When her husband died in the First World War, she had brought them all up on her own. A fiercely independent woman, she claimed to have been the first girl in Banbury to have ridden a bicycle. Lenny's dad was her youngest sibling when still fashionable to treat little boys as little girls, by way of dressing them into the fashion of the day. Lenny and Jean were always fascinated by the framed photo of their dad, which took pride of place at London Road.

Lenny's Grandma started to come and stay over a couple of days a week, then at weekends Lenny and Jean would go to stay at Grandma's house, 218 London road Coventry. Dad took this opportunity to go and watch Coventry City play football. Lenny liked being at Grandma's house playing in the back garden where there was an Anderson air raid shelter, which his dad had installed during the war, with camouflage of dog roses covering it. Lenny and Jean loved to get inside with a supply of brandy snaps to eat and dandelion and burdock for drink to sustain their fantastical journeys.

After a while Dad realised this arrangement must have been a bit of a strain on Grandma so Dad decided to take Lenny with him to watch Coventry City play football at Highfield road. Lenny became an instant fan and begged his dad to take him to the home fixtures. His dad would take Lenny and sit him on a metal barrier behind the goal, under the big clock. It was a great position to get close up action of the goalkeeper diving left to right and getting really muddy. Coventry City's goalkeeper became Lenny's favourite player, his name was

Arthur Lightning. Lenny was so keen to get Arthurs autograph that his dad agreed he could get over the wall and run on the pitch to obtain it.

Unfortunately the match that Lenny chose to obtain Arthurs autograph Coventry had come out to warm up and taken the opposite end to where Lenny was standing. Never mind, over the wall went Lenny in his gabardine mackintosh and ran the full length of the pitch to get Arthurs autograph, the loudest cheers reserved for when Lenny crossed the centre circle. Lenny returning via the perimeter of the pitch clutching his prized possession was escorted by a policeman, who lifted him over the wall in line with the big clock to be reunited with dad. Dad recounted this story many times which he found most entertaining.

During week days, Grandma would stay over quite often at Lenny's house in Kenilworth. Lenny would help her poss the laundry and put it through the mangle, then hang it out on the line. Grandma had a daughter called Olive who ran a guest house at 65 Avondale Road Gorleston-on-sea. It was 165 miles away near Yarmouth. Auntie Olive invited the family to come and celebrate Christmas for which Lenny and Jean where most excited, but how to get there?

Petrol had only recently come off rationing due to the Suez crisis and not many people owned cars. But Dad being Dad was doing out work at that time and had got hold of an old three wheel box van which he used to transport machine parts. It was a Reliant Regent, fitted with an Austin Seven side valve Engine. The front end was a kind of motor bike set up, additionally incorporating two passenger seats, plus a steering wheel. The rear end consisted of a two wheel axle frame supporting an aluminium box, but to Lenny and Jean it was their fantastic, 'Dream-Machine.'

Picture 8: Dream Machine. Three Wheel Box Van.

It had been particularly cold and the week before Christmas Dad discovered that the engine block on the van had cracked, he must have 'forgot about the anti-freeze,' this oversight seemingly putting pay to their Christmas plans. But Dad had other ideas!

He got the van down by the house bay window and rigged up a lead light so he could see to work. He worked on it through the night and got the cast iron engine block off. In the morning Dad tied the engine block to the underside of his crossbar and rode off to Coventry. Two days later the block returned on Dad's bike having been repaired and re-bored. There just left the small matter of fitting the engine back together. Dad needed Lenny to help him to lower the four cylinder cast iron block

Picture 9: Blackie, Jean, Lenny.

down over the pistons. Dad rigged up a sling around the engine block and pushed a broom handle through it to pivot on the bulkhead giving plenty of leverage. Lenny could now control it with ease and lowered the block down to Dad's instructions. With the pistons and rings safely guided in Dad was satisfied he could continue alone. He worked all the hours required in the freezing cold to get the van up and running, not forgetting the anti-freeze!

The day after Dad broke up for the Christmas holiday the family got ready to depart for Gorleston-on-sea. Lenny enquired if Grandma was coming, Dad said 'yes,' 'where is she going to sit?' asked Lenny; Dad got an old armchair out of the garage and put it in the back of the van, 'that's the seat for Grandma,' 'But what about Blackie,' 'Oh' Dad said 'He'll find a lap.' They all readied them selves with plenty of layers of coats and jumpers as the van had no heater and only had canvas side windows, Grandma had a woollen blanket to put over her knees and wore the obligatory hat. Then Dads parting shot was, 'hold your hats on and off we go!

During the journey they did encounter heavy snow and Dad struggled to keep control, it took about eight hours with

Grandma bouncing about in the back. Lenny and Jean had a great Christmas and Lenny got a pair of red roller skates. The promenade at Gorleston-on-sea was long and smooth, ideal for budding skaters. Their return trip was less eventful as the weather was more favourable. But it still took six hours.

Dad decided to make some improvements to the van by way of fitting in some side windows so Grandma could have a clear view out. Then when spring came the family were able to get out and picnic, visiting places of interest. Dad had heard about some mysterious old stones that lay in the middle of a field and thought it might be worth a visit. They were the only ones there and had to climb over a barbed wire fence, leaving Grandma sat in the van. She liked to stay near her chamber pot and couldn't possibly have managed the fence. The kids found it great fun hiding between the enormous boulders, but Blackie sniffed them out every time. Dad said it was called Stonehenge.

Another picnic took the family to Whipsnade Zoo which the kids liked because of all the different animals. Then there was Windsor with a lovely Castle, and as they were so close to London Dad suggested going in to visit an old friend who lived there, which Lenny and Jean found most exciting. Unfortunately nobody answered the door so Dad said to pop a note through the letterbox saying they had called and would come again another day; Blackie left his calling card on one of the boot scrapers. After taking some refreshments then folding away the picnic table they took a look at some of London's landmarks before starting their return journey through Marble Arch to join Watling Street which Dad said would cover over 100 miles. It had been a long day and everybody fell asleep on the way home, except Dad.

Picture 10: Notingate. Jean, Lenny.

Having been away for some time Lenny and Jean's mother returned one day, as suddenly as she had left. Lenny was first to the door and straight into his mother's arms. Somehow she and their father managed to get their marriage back on track, and shortly after she came home they had an announcement: a new baby was on the way. This was something of a surprise, as Mum and Dad were already in their forties, but it was accepted as the good news that it was.

Mum must have been doing some forward planning, when the offer of H.P. and a low weekly payment arrived in the shape of a door to door salesman. Mum signed up on the step for a brand-new twin tub washing machine. Nappies taken care of and no more mangle, must have been the objective. When Lenny got home he marvelled at the brand-new appliance, and excited to see his dad's reaction when he got home from work. No such marvelling from Dad, he dragged the twin tub out and unceremoniously dumped it in the back yard, breaking off one of the wheels. That's what Dad thought of H.P. and the twin tub would have to wait.

Picture 11: Vauxhall Velox.

A more pressing priority for Dad seemed to be upgrading the family transport system from three wheels to four. Dad spotted an advertisement in the used car section of The Coventry Evening Telegraph, from a doctor for the sale of a Vauxhall Velox, one careful owner. Dad took it for a satisfactory test drive then struck a deal to become the proud new-owner of OKV 958. Lenny thought it was magnificent the colour was racing green with loads of chrome and white wall tyres. The interior comforts were equally impressive, leather bench seats front and rear, column change gears with overdrive, radio and heater. This would be traveling in some stile, 'don't forget about the anti-freeze!' Lenny said, Dad replied, 'Ok Len, Ok.'

Dad, eager to put the four wheels into action suggested a picnic. So one Sunday afternoon the car was loaded up with sandwiches drinks and a whole cooked chicken. As they neared the picnic area Dad had a surprise in store as he took the slip road down onto newly constructed M1 motorway. 'Let's see what it can do' said Dad, as it speeded up they found they had some company but not another vehicle as traffic was very light in those early days the company was an express train which tracked along side of the motorway it was so exciting for Lenny and Jean waving at the express and out pacing it. The return to the picnic area was conducted at a more leisurely pace.

That winter, the year of 1963, was the coldest in Britain in living memory. The snow lasted for months, and it was a very hard time for anyone who found it difficult to pay for the huge amount of coal and paraffin needed to keep homes warm. But for the children of Kenilworth playing 'off-piste' on Abbey Fields was a wonderful time, and provided them with some of the happiest memories of their childhoods, chapped legs included. Lenny was no exception.

The summer of 1963 was a very important time for Lenny's family, Mum had been back about a year and she was getting close to having a baby, so the safe delivery of a Hotpoint Twin Tub was most welcome. Lenny's older sister Jean was born in a general hospital and had contracted pneumonia, she was touch and go for two weeks but luckily pulled through. This prompted Dad to have his second child Lenny born in a private nursing home. Lenny's dad wanted to provide the best care available and considering Mums age the nursing home was first choice. July 1963, Julie entered the world, safely delivered by Doctor Harger, Mum always said she liked him!

Mad World

With grammar school out of the question, Lenny graduated from primary school and moved into the local secondary school along with a bunch of his friends. The school, housed in a series of rickety old buildings, was called Castle High. The children used now defunct air raid shelters for their changing rooms. The students were streamed in five groups according to academic ability and Lenny was surprised and pleased to find himself in the middle group – presumably his impressive memory and boyish charm had convinced the teachers that he was more able than he was.

At this point, an influential adult entered Lenny's life in the form of 'Mandy,' a Welsh PE teacher whose real name was Mr Davis, and who bore the moniker as a nickname because the Profumo affair filled the news and was all the adults talked about. Mandy encouraged Lenny to push himself at sports, and he responded eagerly, performing well in cross-country running, but Mandy had no interest in football. 'Football is for sissies,' he said. 'You lot should all be playing rugby.'

In contrast there was Mr Price who took the boys for games. He talked constantly about football and took the kids into the Abbey Fields to play it on a full size pitch next to the war memorial. The Abbey Fields was the most perfect picturesque venue imaginable for cross-country running, set in rolling hills with a rushing brook and a lake locally known as Joe's Overflow.

Picture 12: Kenilworth War Memorial.

Mandy must have been a bit artistic and produced a beautiful map of the scene, consisting of all the geographical and historical features on a full size blackboard. When Mandy unveiled his masterpiece, the boys where astonished to see the route to be run going straight Joe's Overflow and the rushing brook. 'There we are' said Mandy, 'two laps and you will be timed.' This was a regular weekly event and Lenny done well setting the fastest time which was displayed along with his name on Mandy's masterpiece, for all to see. Lenny was so proud of this achievement.

When summer came Mandy expressed another side to his sporting preference which was cricket. On this particular day Lenny was batting and set at the crease, Mandy got a bit fed up with Lenny hogging the batting so he bowled a full toss which hit Lenny on his middle stump, he had to retire to everyone's amusement. They where not supplied with boxes! Lenny and his good friend of many years Jim Tibbets decided to experiment with some field sports, but their unconventional approach of throwing the javelin at each other rather than the traditional method landed them with an unplanned visit to Mr Allenby's office for the inevitable cane. Jim held the record for the most visits to the office which was thirteen!

Sports aside, Lenny didn't like secondary school. The teachers seemed to be determined to fit every square peg into a round hole. Discipline often took the form of a rigorous caning and the atmosphere was not one conducive to personal development. Secondary school had also meant moving out of the relatively protective environment of a rather small Victorian primary school to a situation in which young people from all over Kenilworth were educated together, including the kids growing up on the local council estate and in surrounding villages, and children who arrived from Coventry in two brown double decker buses. This all created a rather tough environment in which bullying and roughhousing were very much the norm.

On the plus side, there were some new friends. Lenny had his first girlfriend, one of the Utley twins (he was never sure which, as they were identical) and he palled around with a lad called Keith Beaufoy, who hailed from Coventry. Lenny and Keith managed to pester their parents into allowing them to go on an unsupervised camping trip to Stratford-on-Avon. The campsite was located at a village called Tiddington on the left bank of the River Avon about a two mile walk from the centre of Stratford. It was Easter time and it turned out to be particularly cold, with ice forming on the tents and cars freezing up. Lenny and Keith made friends with two girls from Liverpool who where older than them.

The girls where really cool and knew all about the Beatles and most proud of the fact that were taking the world by storm. The girls had travelled down to Stratford in a Ford Popular driven by their brothers, for a Shakespearerience. The brothers went off to do their own thing and left the girls to do theirs. The girls had their own bell tent and complained how cold it was.

Lenny and Keith and the two girls got their heads together and worked on ways to keep warm. The first idea was to walk into Stratford and eat fish and chips from Shakespeare's chip shop. The second idea was to go into the local Shakespeare cinema, the film showing was called, It's A Mad, Mad, Mad, Mad, World. They could cuddle up in the cinema and keep warm. The third idea was to sleep together. They did this for three nights on the trot. When it came time for the girls to depart the brothers tried to start their car, it was found that the water pump had frozen. They must have forgotten about the anti-freeze! The brothers said the water pump needed some heat on it, so Lenny got his paraffin primas stove fired up and placed it under the water pump. After about twenty minuets all was well and they went on their way.

During the second year of high school Lenny changed buildings and teachers. When Lenny transgressed he was sent to the headmaster Mr Jeremy nick name Grunt because he grunted when he hit you it was three of the best via a short stubby cane.

The discipline must have been working as Lenny found himself in the top half of the class. When it came to sports day Lenny competed in the 800 yards, his preference was to run barefoot, when he came into the finishing straight he took the lead and didn't look back the applause seemed deafening he had beaten the whole the second and third years combined.

Sport wasn't all plane sailing though when Lenny crossed a tough all action sports master named Ernie Holland he seemed to like dishing C.P. out which he administered with a length of stiff hose pipe. He ordered his victims to bend over and take it on the bum. Lenny had fallen foul of Ernie once before and received three wakes which left marks and was most painful humiliating C.P. that he had ever experienced. This day Ernie court Lenny coming in the changing rooms without first taking off his boots. Ernie got his favourite length of pipe and ordered Lenny to bend over. Lenny declined the invitation which resulted in a stand off, who would blink first, then Ernie dismissed the transgression on this occasion but Lenny was sure that Ernie would not forget.

At around this time, all of Lenny's grandparents passed away, giving the period a general air of instability and flux. Lenny heard some very interesting news: a new school was going to open up in town, catering to both boys and girls. Apparently it was going to be the latest thing in terms of educational philosophy. All the buildings would be shiny and new. Most importantly, there would be no canings whatsoever, a new way of *Educating Kenilworth* to be founded on an approach that abhorred corporal punishment.

Lenny didn't need to think twice; he was in.

Picture 13: ChoirTeam on Parliament Piece. Lenny front row.

Choir Practise

Less than a mile away from Kenilworth Town Centre there is a field called Parliament Piece, said to be where Henry 3rd held the parliament in August 1266. More importantly, in 1963 there were some great conker trees and a full size football pitch.

Lenny learned that the pitch was used and maintained by Saint Nicholas' Boys' Club, which was run by Mr Eric Teale and had a team that played in the under-16 Coventry Choristers' League, with home games being played on a Saturday afternoons on Parliament Piece. Lenny was desperate to play in a real team, so he decided to do what it took to get in. He had to join the church choir and attend choir practice and church once a week on a Sunday, as well as being available for special occasions – despite the fact that he was a Catholic and this was a Church of England club. In return for all that, choristers were paid half a crown a month.

Lenny was issued with an ill-fitting cassock and white dog collar and told to wear black trousers and polished black shoes. On this occasion he found himself in a bit of trouble, an eagle-eyed parishioner spotted Lenny wearing his new baseball boots under his cassock instead of polished black shoes which led to a ticking off, from the curate.

Most of the kids were fourteen or fifteen, and Lenny was twelve. Despite the age difference, he was put on the team and usually played upfront, which was fun because he got to score goals. One match in Coventry at Caludon Castle Park, Lenny was told to man mark a player on the other team, which meant staying between him and your own goal while shadowing his every move. At the end of the match Lenny learned that the boy was the league's top goal scorer – and that he'd prevented him from scoring!

The lads on the team had to work hard to prepare their pitch for matches, marking lines with sawdust and removing all the cowpats from the grass. Dads never came except for once, when there was a dads-versus-lads match. Lenny slide-tackled his father and knocked him to the ground near the corner flag.

The club was affiliated to the F.A. which meant that it was allotted two F.A. Cup Final tickets to distribute. In 1964, Lenny was the lucky one and got to go to the Wembley Stadium to watch West Ham United versus Preston North End in front of a crowd of 100.000. West Ham won 3-2. Bobby Moore was the captain of West Ham and Geoff Hurst scored. Two years later, in the 1966 World Cup final, these two players would become legends.

Not long afterwards the goal posts at Parliament Piece were vandalised and the club was resigned from the league for the rest of the season – but while he was disappointed, Lenny consoled himself with other interests; table tennis being one, the boss selected him to play in the club team which played in a mans league.

The boss would pick him up on his Triumph Tina motor scooter accompanied by his friend Roger Potts driving a Lambretta with his passenger, which made up the team of four. Lenny really enjoyed playing in the league team and often didn't get back home until 10pm.

One of the more unusual activities provided by the club was a potato growing competition. All the boys were allocated a small plot of land at the rear of the Parochial Church Hall in which to plant one seed potato, this year Lenny won the competition with a crop, weighting in at three and three quarter pounds. Walter would have been proud!

The Boy's Club Association was still a strong movement during the 1960's and encouraged boys to participate in outdoor pursuits such as provided by the Duke of Edinburgh awards. An application was made on Lenny's behalf for a place on Outward Bound and he was lucky enough to be accepted.

In competition with the boys club was a newly opened youth centre in Bertie Road. The layout seemed really mod with a split level coffee bar and sunken dance floor, flashing lights and pop music, and Girls. You had to be fourteen to enter which was no problem for Lenny as he had just met this requirement however most of his friends where still just thirteen and tree quarters. There was no strict check on the qualifying age and if you said you where fourteen you where in.

Friday night was club night so Lenny and his cool friends decided to go. Lenny headed the gang confidently stating his age as fourteen which gained him entrance. His friends followed one by one all claiming the qualifying age and being allowed in. When it got to the last lad Paul who was asked his age, he was the boy who couldn't lie he replied thirteen and was refused entrance, then promptly burst into tears!

The youth centre didn't seem to have the structured activities that the boys club provided but there was more freedom and you didn't have to go to choir practice. When February arrived the centre put on a valentines disco Lenny found he was the happy recipient of fourteen valentine cards and had quite a few slow dances!

A chance meeting at the club with an old friend Kevin Terry brought an invitation to join a football team called Kenilworth United. Kevin's dad was the manager and their home ground was in Abbey Fields, Lenny had a good season with Kenilworth United and became top goal scorer with regular write ups in the local paper.

There was a team in Lenny's league called the Baptist's and they were top of the table with a 100% point's tally they had to play one more game and if they won it they would have achieved an unprecedented and historic fete of 100% points total for the whole season. There was a write up about it in the local paper and the only thing standing between them and the historic record was the final game against Kenilworth United.

The venue for the fixture was the Beehive Hill ground and it seemed like the whole town had turned out to watch. The Baptist's took a two goal lead and were already starting to celebrate but then Lenny struck twice hitting one on the turn and crashing in a header from a corner, final score 2-2. This was a very proud occasion for Lenny who had dented the Baptist's and cut out the match report from the local paper and vowed to keep it forever.

Lenny had got himself noticed by the boss of the Baptist's Brian Warr who approached Lenny to join his club, which Lenny accepted and then found himself the youngest player in the side. Baptist's went on to win the Warwickshire cup final with Lenny playing a pivotal roll and being described in the local newspaper as the midfield destroyer.

Football was a huge part of Lenny's life. He had been to a cup final at Wembley and people were already talking about

Picture 14: Gordon Jones. Middlesbrough Captain.

who would get to represent England when she hosted the World Cup in 1966. Lenny's cousin Gordon Jones got selected to play for England, the match was at Villa Park and Gordon played alongside Terry Venables. Before the game Gordon gave Lenny some complimentary tickets, then after the game he gave Lenny his England shirt. Lenny couldn't have been more excited. In those days, a real England football shirt was a rare commodity indeed and very valuable. He knew that he'd been given something that would really impress his mates at school, and vowed that he would keep it forever. Nobody loved football more than Lenny, and everyone knew it. Dad, who wasn't particularly demonstrative or indulgent, had surprisingly given in to Lenny's pleading and had taken him to see the incredible George Best play at Birmingham City. It was a matter of huge pride to Lenny that everyone in school knew that he was a good footballer and loved to see his name in the newspaper.

Newspapers where an important part of everyday life during the 1960's, used for lighting the fire wrapping up of fish and chips tearing into six inch squares and hanging on the back of the toilet door and a source of income. Lenny got his first job which was as a newspaper delivery boy. The news agency he worked for was a little shop on Castle Hill opposite Little Virginia, were it is said that Sir Walter Raleigh planted the first potatoes brought to England. It all started off so well with a weekly salary of twelve shillings and six pence.

Lenny's first investment was to purchase a bicycle rack to make it easier to transport his bundle for delivery. His round incorporated the historic part of Kenilworth and also a modern development of new build houses. As the months passed Lenny's round grew each time a new build house became occupied. It wasn't easy when one winter there was heavy snow and the boy's couldn't use their bicycles but were still expected to trudge round and complete the delivery.

At another ward in Kenilworth there was a news agency called Forboys who where recruiting paper boy's with the offer of fifteen shillings a week. Lenny went along with a good C.V. and was taken on. With higher weekly salary Lenny was able to purchase his first open spool fishing reel and a pair of jeans.

Always keen to get some extra money during his spare time Lenny would do a morning shift at the local farm washing eggs for which he would receive five shillings and ten very numb fingers as the eggs had to be washed in cold water. When he returned home he used to put his hands inside his sisters nappy dryer to warm them up and experienced the most uncomfortable pins and needles imaginable.

Lenny's dad was a good provider for anything he needed but if it was considered a luxury he would have to buy it from his own earnings. One of his higher paid jobs but only seasonal was potato picking however it provided some extra income. While picking potatoes a girl called Janet court Lenny's eye and he invited her to go to the cinema to watch the latest film called Goldfinger staring James Bond. She accepted his offer and they travelled to Coventry on the top deck of a double decker bus disembarking close to the Paris Cinema. Goldfinger was dazzling in its technical ingenuity and they both enjoyed the highly acclaimed film while holding hands.

Top of Lenny's wish list for Christmas of 1964 was a transistor radio and Father Christmas obliged with a Ferguson 358BT, eight inch portable earpiece included. The transistor radio became the most popular communication device in history with millions being manufactured during the 1960's. Their pocket size sparked change in popular music listening habits allowing people to listen to music wherever they went. Transistors had only recently been developed for the mass-market and the transistor radio became one of the must have gadgets of the 1960's.

Often in the news where story's of a radio station called Caroline transmitting from a pirate ship off the east coast playing all the latest must not listen to pop music. Lenny's cousin, Billy Shanks from Yarmouth received a strong signal from Caroline and enjoyed all the new records but Lenny was disappointed not to be able to tune in as the signal wasn't strong enough in the Midlands so he had to be contented with radio Luxembourg. There was a weekly chart show on Luxembourg and Lenny used to tape it on his dads reel to reel tape recorder to play back his favourite records time and time again for pleasure.

Lenny's dad put another black and white television in the front room, so the kids could watch Crackerjack and Doctor Who, along with all their favourite programs without disturbing him. 'Top of the Pops' was a new ground breaking program featuring all the latest music and fashion it was a much looked forward to and talked about weekly event. Lenny's older sister's friend used to come round and watch the show, she wore a fashionable nylon polo neck top which was figure hugging and made her breasts most visible. Lenny found her breasts most interesting and used to sit next to her on the settee where she let him touch them while watching the latest pop stars including the Beatles and Rolling Stones.

Saturday night was a bit special as far as Lenny was concerned left to babysit his little sister, while Mum and Dad went ballroom dancing. He prepared himself a full pot of tea, with his fisherman's mug at the ready to dunk a whole packet of chocolate digestive biscuits while watching 'Match of the Day.'

Brand New Everything

Although very few of Lenny's friends and classmates made the move to the new Abbey High school, his parents were happy with the change of scene. The school was predominantly middle-class on the golf club side of town, with a pinch of back to backs surrounded by farmland greenbelt and a cricket club it was perfect for Lenny less than a mile bike ride to Leyes Lane.

Dad seemed to be positively delighted; he rushed out and bought Lenny a brand-new leather satchel and Slazenger duffle-bag to use, and a new uniform was purchased from J. A. Moores gentleman's outfitter established 1903 who supplied the best quality uniform available, there was a cheaper version obtainable from the Co-Op.

Lenny was quite excited about starting at the new school. Now an adolescent, he was increasingly aware of his educational difficulties and hoped that the new school would also be a new start. Knowing that the facilities would all be brand-new, the latest thing in modernity, he also presumed that the sports facilities would be amazing, and couldn't wait to get to grips with them.

The first day at the new school everything seemed thrilling it was September 6th 1965, and the doors were 'swinging' open. Having always been educated in ramshackle old buildings, it was tremendously exciting for Lenny to walk into a purpose-built new school in which everything was untarnished. It felt like being the first person to walk across a fresh field of virgin-snow. To be first is something very special and produced a memory that would last forever.

All the pupils were received in the main school hall where they were placed with a form teacher, Lenny somewhat surprisingly found himself in the top form along with a few friends their teacher was Miss Mansfield. All the teachers where then invited to join Miss Dorothy Parncutt on stage where she introduced herself as the headmistress to a very wide eyed audience. It could not go unnoticed by wearing a figure hugging top making her look like something off a saucy sea side postcard she instantly acquired the nickname of Buckets.

After the formal introduction was completed the pupils where given a guided tour of the school by their form teachers. Impressive indeed was the canteen which had all the latest equipment and utensils to cook all the meals on site chips included. All the previous schools attended by Lenny had their school dinners delivered in large aluminium trays or flasks and had gained a reputation of being less than a la carte. It was also pointed out that there was to be a tuck shop run by the pupils selling crisps, jammy dodgers and wagon wheels washed down with free school milk.

The tour continued visiting rooms for art, home economics, science then two amazing workshops housing unmarked benches a forge hammers and tongs drilling machines and razor sharp chisels all sparkling in the sunbeams of September. Framed by the workshop window was a view into an outsized car park accommodating just two old bangers one car was a Morris Minor convertible with a tatty old hood owned by the new games teacher Miss Lazel she didn't have a nickname she was just plane Ann. The second car was an Austin A40 Farina owned by Mandy who had also transferred to the new school, he always boasted his cars top speed. He would say 'Do the ton Lenny, do the ton,' the lads very much doubted it.

Finely back in the school hall the class was guided through a passageway leading to changing rooms, perfect indeed with hot shower's, off the changing rooms was an exit onto the playing fields.

Initial excitement gave way to crushing disappointment when it was revealed that the new playing fields could not be used as they had just been seeded, also there was no gymnasium it gradually became apparent that sports were not exactly a priority for the headmistress, Dorothy Parncutt, who was a well-known local educator who had just resigned her post from a large girls' school in Coventry that was about to be merged with a large boys school to form a mixed comprehensive in line with government policy.

It must have seemed an attractive once in a life time offer for the middle aged Dorothy to lead the small mixed brand-new high school in leafy Kenilworth which was that kind of town just waiting for something to happen this was to be a brave new experiment in *Educating Kenilworth*, where she could apply her own personal stamp.

During the settling in period it was confirmed that there would be no canings or corporal punishment what so ever, well almost, bad behaviour would be dealt with by means of a conduct sheet system. The conduct sheet had the week's timetable on it and each period would have to be signed off by a teacher to indicate good behaviour if all the boxes where signed that was the end of the sheet if not it would be detention. There was also to be a reward system by the way of tallys. A tally was a small piece of wood about one inch square by a quarter inch thick with a brightly coloured surface a red tally was of the highest value and most coveted. These where handed out for high achievement and good behaviour, rewards took the form of free periods and prizes.

It was brought to the boy's attention that the length of hair permitted must not descend below the top of their shirt collars, and caps must be worn at all times when traveling to and from school. A strict dress code would be monitored and failure to comply would result in a conduct sheet.

It was the 1960s and everything seemed to be changing. Young people were increasingly beginning to challenge their parents' assumptions and the very nature of British society was transforming as the last remnants of the Empire disappeared. In this context it was increasingly apparent that there was an urgent need to educate young people differently and in a way that would equip them for the new world that they were going to live in.

Lenny's new school brought with it the promise of change and of an approach to education that would be completely new and very different to everything else on offer in Kenilworth. The students were told that they could elect a head boy and head girl, and Lenny was thrilled when he was chosen. Along with the role came the position of chairman of the school committee, with the head girl as his secretary. For a fourteen year old boy it was all tremendously exciting.

The uniforms at the new school were a bit ridiculous – they were modelled on what the girls had worn at the Dorothy's former school and the boys looked very silly in their bright red caps and the girls where most noticeable in their bright red blazers – but that seemed like a small price to pay for what promised to be an exciting new approach to education.

That first day of school, and most days after that, Dorothy arrived in a taxi that had brought her all the way from Coventry, together with Miss Mansfield and the daughter of one of her friends (the head girl – all the students assumed that the vote had been rigged in her favour and considered her Dorothy's pet). Many of the new teachers on the staff had worked for her at the previous school too and they formed a sort of cabal – they set the tone and the atmosphere at the school and heaven help any pupil or member of staff who tried to intervene!

Cross-Country Champ

At first, things seemed to be going reasonable well. The lack of sports facilities was disappointing, but Lenny was determined to make school work out, and to do as much physical activity as possible. Instead of a sports master and it came as a bit of a surprise to the lads they where going to be taken for games by a lady, a tall woman named Ann Although the pupils where not happy with the fact that the playing fields could not be used it was not the teachers fault, the general felling was why not a woman lets give it a go.

The main sports available were cross-country running or cross-country running. If it was a single period the boys would run the big O course which was about two miles covering lanes and farm land. If it was a double period they would run the figure of eight course, which was about four miles long. This course cutting through Glasshouse Woods passing the golf course and the hunted house in Crew Lane to join up with the big O course to completion. Ann would wait at the school gate to welcome the returning boys and Lenny was always first. On one occasion Lenny put in a particularly quick time with Ann no where to be seen so Lenny made his usual way around passed the work shops and peeped in to see the metal work teacher smoking and Ann in good mood. Lenny passed quietly by and went to enjoy a hot shower.

Lenny was entered into Mid-Warwickshire cross-country

running competition to be held at Myton School in Warwick, he had to go over to Leamington on his own and walk two miles to the venue in Warwick. He had a number pinned on his shirt then the flag dropped and off they went. The route was along the Myton road in view of Warwick castle up the Banbury road to Heathcote Lane across two potato fields then back into the grounds of Myton High. Lenny did his best and came third, the numbers from their shirts where recovered by officials to compile the results list. Then came the official announcement in first place in Lenny's age group was Lenny, who thought there had been some sort of clerical error but after his enquiry it was explained that the two lads who had fronted his race where in a different age group. Lenny was absolutely delighted to be crowned a Mid-Warwickshire champion.

Covered from head to toe in thick mud Lenny made his trek back to the Leamington bus station where he boarded and sat on the top deck. On home arrival Lenny was met by his dad who had just finished his Saturday overtime shift seeing Lenny's muddy predicament Dad placed his sister's blue baby bath in the middle of the lawn and Lenny in it where he recounted the result of the race while being hosed down by his dad with cold water. He stayed busy with cross-country running despite the fact that nobody from school or home had turned out to see him win it was one of the proudest moments of his young life.

In school, Lenny was starting to realise that things weren't as perfect as he'd hoped. The principal seemed to feel that the best way to educate boys was to treat them as if they were girls. During a hard winter period it was felt to dangerous for the lads to go out road running so they where coached in the art of netball and when the weather got even worse they learned square dancing in the assembly hall with the girls. Lenny thought this was alright, quite exciting as it brought the opposite sex into close physical contact, but it didn't suit everybody.

Lenny was also increasingly distracted by girls – and he was beginning to be quite successful with them. Sexual attraction and feelings were never discussed by the teachers, leaving the students to sort out everything on their own. The results of this oversight were predictable.

Out of the Box

Dorothy's brave new idea for an exchange trip with a school in London when announced in assembly and met with great excitement and enthusiasm from Lenny as he had never been involved in anything quite like it. He pleaded with his dad to let him go and he got the green light. A check list was sent home with the participant trippers for them to prepare their suitcases.

Lenny had most of the required kit for the trip but was lacking a pair of slippers. So Dad gave him some money and he went over on the bus to the Coventry round market believed to be the only one of its kind in Europe and bought a brown and badged checked pair of slippers ready for packing.

Dad dug out the loft an old dark blue suitcase which looked ok when all the cobwebs and dust was cleaned off, he said it was the one he used when traveling between aerodromes during the war. Packing was fun putting everything in and out many times till the best lie was found. Finely packed Dad thought it best to put one of his old leather belts around it in case it burst open during transit.

The pupils where told that they would each be paired off with a pupil from the High School of Sidcup in Kent. Lenny was placed with the head boy of year three, before the trip would take place instructions where given to write each other a brief letter of introduction.

The big day came and Lenny lugged his suitcase all the way

to school it wasn't easy, the pupils going on the exchange trip assembled in the main school hall to be spoken to by Dorothy. She explained this was the first ever school trip and a historic moment of which she was very proud and the pupils where all ambassadors. After Dorothy's pep talk they took out all their cases and put them on the coach. Then off, down passed Lenny's house on to the A45 along to the M45 then down the M1 waving at all the traffic everybody very excited at the prospect of seeing some of London's land marks. It turned out to be a particularly wet period and they couldn't see much but it was dry and fun being on the coach away from school. As they got into London expectations where very high but nothing visible of any note was spotted, not even the River Thames as they crossed it was above their heads while in the Blackwall Tunnel.

'It won't be long now,' driver announced and before they knew it the coach pulled up out side Sidcup High. After a several minuets of paused anticipation a small reception party approached the coach headed by a couple of teachers and two pupils who turned out to be the head girl and head boy of year three. The teachers stepped on board and welcomed everybody to Sidcup High and invited them to the school assemble hall.

After disembarkation in full uniform they made their way behind the reception committee into the school, eyes seemed to be peering at them from all angles. Sidcup High didn't wear caps or hats and it appeared as if they where being visited by a load of posh kids, from some public school. For the small town kids of Kenilworth they weren't prepared for how out of place they would feel, but it was still very exciting. Sandwiches and drinks were served then the formal welcome was given.

First impressions where that this was a big school as they had both forth and fifth years placed, the buildings looked functional but knocked about. The kids spoke with London accents and appeared very confident with fashionable hair cuts, both boys and girls seemed very mod and no silly hats. It didn't go unnoticed that the London girls wore their skirts very short compared to the Abbey girls who had to wear theirs below the knees on Dorothy's orders.

All the pupils were then paired off with the kids they had corresponded with. Lenny met his respondent head boy of year three named Terry.

The following morning which was a Friday the Abbey crowd took the coach into London passing over Tower Bridge to a jetty where they boarded a motor boat which ferried them to Traitors Gate then on to the Tower of London. The weather held and they were able to enjoy the Crown Jewels, Beefeaters and chasing the ravens. One teacher remarked what a shame nobody had a camera to make a visual record of this historic trip. Then the Abbey crowd were taken passed Big Ben and the houses of parliament returning to Sidcup. Lenny enjoyed his stay at Terry's house, wearing his new slippers, and looked forward to a game of football scheduled for Saturday morning at Sidcup High prior to their return home. The game was a complete wash out but they managed to have a kick about in the gym which was fun. Before they knew it the Abbey crowd were back on the coach and heading north bound on the M1.

A full report on the trip had to be written and delivered to an excited assembly this was no problem for Lenny as he got his secretary to do it. She confided with Lenny some secret news that the head girl of Sidcup High had a crush on him and was very much looking forward to their visit to Kenilworth Abbey. This was the spring of 1966 and the year had got of to a very good start as far as Lenny was concerned he was enjoying the roll of head boy and being the face of the new school

When a V.I.P. came to the school to deliver a very important message Lenny was entrusted to escort him round to various class rooms and sit through the lecture. It began with him introducing the term Modern Maths and he went on to say that in the future it would change all our lives. Then he gave his demonstration, he said 'This is the most important thing that is going to happen,' Having gained the full attention of the class he walked over to the light switch and turned the lights on then off. Binary system was mentioned and two digits 1 and 0. Nobody had a clue what he was on about but it was fun listening to him Lenny thought he was probably the only pupil that the message stuck with as he had to listen to it several times but had no idea what it meant and wouldn't for many years to come.

Not long after it was time for the return visit of the mods from Sidcup Lenny was really looking forward to them coming up not least in the expectation of a romantic liaison with the head girl. On their arrival they were paraded on the school stage where Lenny opened the introduction ceremony with the head girl from London just behind him, it was quite a warm day so blazers had been put on the back of the chairs revealing her petite figure with generous blouse button busters she got next to Lenny and pushed herself into him but Lenny managed to keep his composure and concluded his welcoming speech with a smile.

The London crowd were going to visit the new and ruined Coventry Cathedrals and on their return they had been given permission for a Friday night out at the Kenilworth youth club. Terry who was staying at Lenny's house had brought with him two fashionable shirts Lenny was delighted when Terry agreed to lend him one to wear for the night out.

When Lenny met up with the head girl from London at the youth club, they found a dark corner where they embraced for most of the evening. That night the Mods from London took over, and showed the young people of Kenilworth how to dance, and it wasn't square. They seemed a cut above with their fashionable hair-dos and knowledge of the latest music and dance. The lid was off the box and blown away, things were 'swinging.' Lenny thought that night that Kenilworth would never be the same again!

These were happy times. Although his academic work was not going well and he had moments of confrontation with the teaching staff, Lenny's life seemed to him to be a joyride. He relished every success in sport and felt as though he was at the centre of a whirlwind of fun. At the school swimming gala organised by Ann, he found himself stranded half way down the lane with his trunks having slipped off and sunk to the tiled bottom of the pool causing quite a stir, he enjoyed being the centre of attention.

It Was Alright

After the exchange trip with London, Lenny was more interested in girls than ever, despite his various duties as the head
boy. Still aged fourteen, he and a girl from his class at school
lost their virginity together at the top of the playing fields
behind the classrooms. He didn't tell anyone, but somehow
the news spread like wildfire and he acquired a reputation as
a man about town. Everyone wanted to know what it had been
like having sex. Lenny reckoned that it was alright.

It was unusual to see parents up at the school and after about
a week or so the mother of the girl that Lenny had been with
appeared visiting Dorothy's office nothing was said but it con-
centrated the mind and gave Lenny plenty to think about. In
assembly the pupils were reminded that the playing fields were
still strictly out of bounds, and the staffroom had been equipped
with a pair of binoculars, presumably to keep a close eye on
the wild life. That first experience didn't exactly develop into
a lasting meaningful relationship but they did subsequently
enjoy several walks in Abbey Fields together holding hands.

In the 1960s young people were at least vaguely aware of a
cultural revolution that was going on around them but their
parents and the educational establishment hadn't caught up.
Some of the young people in school were becoming sexually
active, and the teachers did little to prepare them for a world
that was changing rapidly. Mandy made it clear to Lenny that

he knew what was going on, but there was no sex education or anything like that.

One of the more forward thinking teachers was Mr Price who had transferred from Castle High school to Abbey. Lenny remembered him taking the lads to play football in the Abbey Fields here he took geography which Lenny enjoyed. His lessons about the North American Tundra, and rock formations were very interesting, meandering rivers were also talked about and he pointed out that the meander in a river could actually be viewed from a high vantage point. Apart from his formal duties Mr Price ran a very popular lunch time club where the kids were encouraged to talk about topics of the day and play pop music. Lenny loved talking about football stars which he had seen, such as Bobby Moore and George Best. He thought that some of the best songs where by Cat Stevens and Chris Farlowe, there was also a new group that the mods from Sidcup had mentioned called The Who, Who?

The boys wanted their hair long like the pop stars they seen on T.V. and in magazines far away from their dad's Brylcreem style. This turned out to be a battle ground with barely a day going by without some hair confrontation. If you had it to short you got stick from your class mates and if you had it to long you got a conduct sheet and to top it off you had to wear a silly bright 'red-cap.' What was Dorothy thinking of when she dreamt that one up? The girls had a similar problem with the 60s fashion of short skirts, Dorothy demanded below the knees.

One of Dorothy's inner circle and enforcers of the hem line was a little old lady named Ma Clark, she was as old as the hills, and the only thing she seemed to care about was her plants. The whole length of her classroom window ledge was potted, this made her a target for the lads who devised a saline solution to turn her greenery brown.

Colourful was the art teacher Mrs Clegg old and mad in appearance with little if any idea how to control a class with adolescent boys. Tights were the fashion but Mrs Clegg was stuck in the past with stockings how did the pupils know this bit of highly personal information. It was spotted that one day she was wearing one seamed stocking and one plain stocking the art room was in uproar and would never be the same again.

Lenny usually amused himself in art with his friend James Douglas who liked to remind Lenny that he had given him a back eye when they were at primary school. Together they would draw and paint pictures of motor bikes and dream of what it must be like to be a ton up kid, on a 'Triumph Bonneville.' The art room cupboard had its uses and was very popular when a certain girl would entertain the lads by letting them touch her up when the light was switched off. The art room seemed a bit of a do what you like sort of place to be.

A place where you certainly did not do as you like was the science lab and in total control, woe be-tide anybody who stepped out of line. It was the domain of Mr Miller nicknamed Ned. The lads thought he looked like Max Wall with his tight black trousers long hair with a monk's crown. He was scary, prone to bouts of bad temper and rage. Lenny found science very interesting and tried hard, but not all the kids shared Lenny's enthusiasm. Ned's style was to set some work for the pupils, then walk up and down the gangways between the desks peering over the student's shoulders to examine their work, as he passed by the lads would stick two fingers up behind his back, sitting directly ahead of Lenny was his friend Terry

Shillton and when Ned passed by Terry gave him the salute which Ned spotted in the mirrored reflection of the science lab window, Ned spun round and hit Terry across the face with a force that was lucky not to cause damage, then stormed out the lab leaving a stunned silence behind.

During another science lesson focused on electrical circuits Ned was patrolling the gangways, when he peered over Lenny's shoulder he blew a fuse. Ned stormed off to his table taking something from the draw, returning to Lenny's desk and slamming his hand down when he lifted it there lay two much coveted red tallys. Ned shouted 'You're the only one in this class with any common sense!' The rest of this class would go on to form the first ever fifth year with one exemption, the boy with common sense.

When it came to engaging with adolescent boys, Mr Wolstenholme, the metal work teacher had his own style, his nickname was Bomber he was fresh out of teachers training college with a dry sense of humour. As Lenny had always been good at hand craft and given the fact that his dad was a toolmaker, Lenny took to metal work in a big way. He was eager to learn some new skills like brazing riveting and planishing which is a metal working technique to finely shape sheet metal. Lenny made several pieces of which he was most proud and still uses to this day, achieving high marks from Bomber.

On one occasion the lads were tasked to make a copper bowl with a stand. This required a six inch diameter disc to be cut from a copper sheet one eighth of an inch thick using snips. Then to work the copper by planishing it round and round, till it formed into a bowl, the final stage was to braze on the stand, this took one whole term to complete. When it came to marking the work Lenny was delighted to be graded with a B as most of the lads were given Cs and Ds. The final piece of work to be marked was handed to Bomber who got all the lads round his bench to witness the event. He first asked the lad who had submitted it what grade he thought it was worth, the lad whispered C. Bomber shouted 'Since how long as my work only been worth C.' The lad who handed it in had trashed his own piece then stolen Bomber's demonstration piece and submitted for marking.

Bombers greatest project was an Austin 7 the idea was to get the lads to strip it down and renovate it was great fun pushing each other round then taking it in turns to do the steering.

Lenny's form teacher was Miss Mansfield who was believed to be Dorothy's right hand woman and gained the unfortunate moniker of Thunder-Guts never quite sure why, but she did have a bit of a roar. She took English which was Lenny's most challenging subject and he lagged well behind most of the class and really needed some additional help, but this wasn't spotted, or if it was nothing was said. Lenny found it difficult to concentrate with all the letters appearing to dance about on the page. He would amuse himself listening through his ear piece to his tranny concealed in his satchel. Inevitably Thunder-Guts, caught him at it and confiscated Lenny's tranny, and had his desk moved to the front where she could keep a close eye on his work. There were no lockers or anything like that, theft was unheard of and the only things likely to be taken were by way of confiscations.

Lenny got a new job offer, instead of delivering newspapers and getting bitten by dogs for fifteen shillings a week, he could stay in the warm and mark them up for twenty shillings a week. Marking up meant writing the house numbers and road names on the newspapers ready for the lads to deliver, the only thing was it meant a 6am start. Lenny talked it over with his dad who agreed to let him do the job as long as Lenny got himself up at 5.45am. An alarm clock with big bells on was the answer to that.

It was most interesting for him looking at all the different magazines and supplements that had to be put in to the Sunday news papers, and quite a few were from the top shelf.

Back of the Net

Picture 15: World Cup Willie 1966.

World Cup Willie was the first mascot to be associated with a major sporting event. Willie appeared on badges and memorabilia of the day depicting a lion wearing a union flag. It was 1966 and football fever was taking hold all across England.

Middle England was not to be left out and devised their own World Cup idea to play a football knockout competition between the schools. Abbey received their invitation to participate which was announced to a surprised assembly by Dorothy who was always keen to be patriotic and beat the drum. Lenny was declared captain and handed the mandate to form a team fit for purpose he was to be in charge of all matters football. Returning to his classroom after assembly; digesting the enormity of the task ahead and given the fact that he was now manager coach and captain with no usable football pitch to train or play on.

Lenny was pursued and jostled by a group of girls headed by Linda Cook all shouting and joking that they wanted to be in the team Lenny snapped under the pressure and told them to 'shut up' and slapped Cookie across the face. To a stunned silence Cookie sat down at her desk and sobbed the whole of the next period. Thunder-Guts never enquired why Cookie was sobbing, if she had revealed the reason, it may have resulted in the shortest football managerial appointment of all time. Lenny always deeply regretted his action but never found a way to apologise, Lenny liked Cookie and thought that she should have been head girl.

Although the playing fields were still out of bounds it was hoped that they would become playable sometime soon, but in the mean time the tennis courts would have to do for training. As the days went by Lenny used his personality and football knowledge to form a team. It wasn't easy as some of the better players worked on Saturdays but Lenny managed to persuade enough to take the time off.

Fortunately, because the only sport available at the school had been cross-country running the lads were all extremely fit and Lenny could concentrate on positional play and tactics. Training took place after-school in the tennis courts but the lads were not allowed to use footballs as they would scuff up so they had to use netballs. They played five a side attack, verses defence and a pattern of play was emerging. The lads worked hard but there was no denying the lack of some basic skills. Lenny realised that this was going to have to be a 'tough it out long ball team,' to stand any chance. But what they lacked in skill they were keen to make up for with their enthusiasm and determination.

The fixture list was drawn up for the cup competition and Abbey drew a bye which Lenny thought was fine and would allow themselves more time to prepare. Then Abbey were pitched against a Leamington side that had to cancel so Abbey were awarded the tie and found themselves in the wonderful position of being in the final with a home draw. The team they would play against was none other than Lenny's old school Castle High. This took things to a whole new level. This game wasn't just about Castle High this was about Ernie Holland who Lenny had stood up to once before, this was Ernie's team. The lads knew that Ernie would do all he could to rub their noses in it and trained even harder in preparation for the big day.

After a further wet spell it became apparent that the school playing fields were not going to be ready in time for the cup final Lenny was devastated, after all the hard work the lads had put in. He thought there must be a solution, looking out of Lenny's classroom window could be seen a thick hawthorn hedge directly the other side was a beautiful full size football pitch owned by the Wardens sports club. If only they could get permission to play their World Cup Final on it. Lenny asked Dorothy if he could approach the Wardens with the idea of using their pitch for this one off special she agreed and Lenny got his secretary to write out nothing short of a begging letter requesting permission to use their pitch for this one off match. It worked, 'Game on,' the team couldn't have been more excited and they were supplied with a brand-new red and white kit. 'Wembley beckoned!'

Dorothy's idea of fair play, jolly hockey sticks, and it's the taking part that counts not the winning, just didn't wash with the lads. This game was about winning not the taking part, and putting Abbey on the map, it meant being able to walk the streets of Kenilworth with heads held high even if they did have to wear silly red caps.

Saturday morning World Cup Final, Lenny arrived wearing his England shirt, first job was to liaise with the caretaker and make sure everything was in place for the match. Then welcome the opposition, Ernie bounced off the bus in his silly tracksuit and said 'Take me to your leader,' Lenny replied 'I am the leader,' then showed him round to the changing rooms.

The first half was very tough and Abbey were severely tested but managed to blunt the sharp edge of the opposition. During the second half Abbey were more able to get forward but it remained in deadlock.

With Ten minutes to go it was 0-0 when Lenny headed a ball into the back of the net from a corner swept in by Jim Tibbets and won the game 1-0 to lift the World Cup. Lenny had his secretary make out a full match report for him to deliver the good news to the school assembly. He proudly wore his England shirt to do so and the whole team was paraded on the stage to generous applause from staff and pupils. Against all the odds, they had won. Dared they dream?

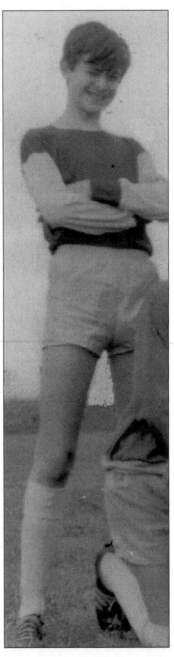

Picture 16: Lenny School Captain 1966.

Eisteddfod

As head boy, chairman of the school committee and captain of the football team, Lenny was supposed to help to disseminate a spirit of discipline and hard work among his fellow students, but the fact was that he found it difficult to do so. This may have been a brand-new school but some of the kids were damaged. Many of the youngsters were naturally quite destructive and they tended to act up. When Lenny found one of his mates vandalising equipment in the woodwork room, for example, he didn't quite know what to do, his friend said proudly, 'come and have a look at this,' he had hammered a woodwork chisel into a brand-new woodwork bench that deep it could not be removed Lenny said, 'what do you think your doing?' to which he replied laughingly, 'it slipped' he knew Lenny wouldn't grass him up but it led to all possible suspects being rounded up for detention.

Everybody there was given a piece of paper and told to write down the name of the vandal then fold it up and put it in a waste paper bin. This system of whistle blowing may have worked perfectly well at Dorothy's old girls school in Coventry but it was never going to work at Abbey, nobody grassed or was likely to. 'It wasn't the way.' A similar event took place in the metal work room which Lenny was a witness to but didn't feel he could say anything about it he began to feel uneasy; he had thought it would all be great fun being the head boy and he had been really happy when his friends had elected him, but he wasn't prepared for this kind of responsibility. He was increasingly aware that the principal and her staff didn't really approve of him, and wished that they had not let the students freely elect one of the boys in what had basically been a popularity contest, and it was not necessarily the right way to find the lad for the job. He often got into trouble, for using 'bad language,' for failing to listen in class, or for another infraction.

The French teacher Miss Williams wore fashionable nylon polo neck tops, purpose being to cover up her love bites, she was very popular, it didn't hurt that she was strikingly good looking and that all the boys had a crush on her. The back row in her class was occupied by some very rosy cheeked lads who had devised a method of personal massage by way of a hole in their pockets. They dared Lenny to feel her bottom as she passed by in the corridor wearing her pencil skirt this could have spelt big trouble, but she ignored the encounter in French style. She was kind to Lenny; he struggled badly in French so she let him do his French project in English. Even when he misbehaved in her class, she did her best to be understanding and reasonable.

On some level, Lenny realised that he was not getting the sort of education he needed at school but, being young and inexperienced, he wasn't able to put into words what he felt he did need, and all the distractions of responsibility had resulted in him falling badly behind where it really counted.

One thing that Lenny was really looking forward to was the playing fields becoming operational that day finely arrived during the summer term of 1966 after a nine month gestation period. First a tractor fitted with gang mowers cut the huge field, a few days later the running track was marked out along with the out field markings. Lenny loved track running and preferred to run barefoot. Now the fields were operational they stopped cross-country running and pursued field sports and tennis. The games teacher Ann, who was always good for a joke, didn't do much in the way of organising the lads who were allowed to please themselves what they did, she liked to be round by the tennis courts where she could flirt with Bomber.

Mandy started an after-school cricket club that Lenny wasn't very interested in but when it came to a match Lenny was asked to play by his mates to make up the number. Lenny had a swing of the bat and made a few runs then when his side was fielding he was out on the boundary. When the last man was out Mandy announced the scores were even both side had scored an equal amount of runs, they said to decide a winner they would have a throw off, which meant each team to select a player and see who could throw the cricket ball the furthest. They threw first then a ball was tossed to Lenny who sent the cricket ball sailing passed the oppositions throw and won the match for Mandy it was all great fun. Lenny liked to remind Mandy that the World Cup wasn't far away and that Lenny had already lifted 'One' but Mandy from Wales maintained that rugby was the real mans game. Lenny's school didn't participate in rugby, for that you had to attend the grammar school.

Lenny was really looking forward to sports day then there was an announcement in assembly that instead of a traditional style sports day it would be replaced with an Eisteddfod – a Welsh-themed day of arts and culture. Lenny reacted to all of this by becoming quite rebellious; he brought a stink bomb to the Eisteddfod and let it off. It was never proven who was behind the horrible stench, but Dorothy had a very good idea.

It was infuriating for Dorothy and the rest of the staff to have to deal with a head boy who was lionised by the rest of the students, but who could be so challenging with adults.

As far as Lenny was concerned the Eisteddfod idea was none starter, but there was one high point. David Bowdler was a good friend of Lenny's and they enjoyed field sports together, in particular the high jump. David was the by far the best musician in the school and artistic, not being able to wear their hair long David came up with the idea of getting a lady's eye pencil and drawing in some sideboards and a moustache. He composed a piece of music which he played at the Eisteddfod to entertain the crowd. He introduced it as 'A Cross-Country Run in Glasshouse Woods by Len Unsworth, it wasn't really it was A walk in the Black Forrest,' which was a bouncy number that sold a million but on this occasion he managed to avoid the copyright.

David's method of rebellion was a little more subtle than Lenny's; he would mimic Thunder-Guts who used to play the piano in assembly, which at best could be described as badly. When she dropped a note she would look round to see if anybody had noticed, David would mimic this by playing a popular tune and dropping notes. It was thought this was where Les Dawson got the idea for his T.V. show.

Summer of 66

Picture 17: VW Beetle 1966.

The summer of 1966 was an absolutely glorious one in all of Britain. Lenny's dad got a bright red brand-new Beetle, 1200cc air cooled engine, 'no anti-freeze required,' with extras (fitted radio and continental bumpers for the all in price of £600!) Lenny's older sister Jean had passed her O levels and had been accepted at Leamington College for Girls to study for her A Levels. Lenny and his mate John Tallis got the green light to go on an unsupervised camping trip to Stratford-on-Avon for a whole week.

Lenny and John were dropped off at Tiddington which was just outside Stratford and had a campsite on the left bank of the River Avon. While the camp was being set up it was on with the transistor radio to listen to the latest pop songs and the Kinks drifted across the site with their hit song, 'Sunny Afternoon,' which couldn't have been more appropriate. Then out with the fishing tackle. River fishing was different to what the lads were used to because of the flowing water, but they soon got to grips with using a leger. The campsite had a jetty next to the river with a small rowing boat moored for campers to use there was also a camp shop and café.

In stark contrast to Lenny's previous visit to the site when it was freezing, this time it was the opposite end of the thermometer and tents can get very hot. So it was on with the trunks and jumping off the jetty into the river for a swim to cool down where Lenny got friendly with a girl from the new town of Peterlee County Durham, she was camping with her parents. This was Tuesday the 26th of July 1966 and Lenny invited her for a romantic meal in the campsite café followed by a punt up the river, then they returned to Lenny's tent to listen to his transistor radio, the result was amazing England beat Portugal to reach the World Cup Final. The couple vowed to keep in touch and exchanged addresses.

The morning of Saturday the 30th of July 1966 had finely arrived and Dad came to pick up the lads to get them home in time to see the World Cup Final. Everyone was glued to their televisions or their transistor radio's this was to be the most amazing day in England's sporting history.

Lenny sat on the settee with Blackie, the family pet poodle, in front of a black and white television and soaked up the

Picture 18: Bobby Moore England Captain 1966.

pressure as the pendulum swung first one way then the other, at half time Lenny even started biting his nails which he had never done before in his life; even Mum looked in to see how it was going. Finely, after extra time England had beaten West Germany 4-2. Bobby Moore the captain of England lifted the World Cup this was a day that would never be forgotten. Life was wonderful for Lenny and he barely had time to get his breath back and he was off on Outward Bound.

The course centre was on the outskirts of the picturesque village of Ambleside on the north shore of Lake Windermere. The centre was too good to be true encompassing all activities imaginable. There were sixty lad's inducted on the course from all over the country. Lenny had never spoken to anybody of a different colour to himself before but instantly palled up with a lad called Livingston Rickets who hailed from London. Livingston and Lenny formed an attacking partnership to spearhead their volleyball team. The boys were split into four teams of fifteen with two instructors per team. All the lads had to conquer England's highest mountain called Scafell Pike standing at 3210ft.

Unexpectedly introduced was an artistic side to the course. It was announcement that the boys were to perform a play entertaining a live audience from the local village of Ambleside. The play to be performed would be a contemporary version of 'The Hound of the Baskervilles' staring Sherlock Holmes, who is a fictional detective. Lenny didn't volunteer to be in the cast but found himself pushed into the lead roll of Sherlock Holmes. All the lines had to be learned, makeup applied, and props at the ready; the play was performed without a hitch apart from a bit of prompting which only added to the amusement of the audience. It was quite an achievement by the young stars and met with warm applause and three encores.

After the show a reception party was laid on for the audience and cast to enjoy. Attending the party was the local Carnival Queen who got together with Lenny. Later that evening after a couple of slow dances she invited him to come back and stay the night at her cottage as her parents were away and only had the company of her older sister.

Lenny was keen to take her up on the offer but couldn't see a way of getting leave from the Outward Bound Centre. Livingston had the solution he would cover for him by placing some pillows in his bunk, Lenny went A.W.O.L. The plan worked perfectly with Lenny returning at 5-30 in the morning climbing through the open kitchen window that had been left for him, 'Elementary.' The anxieties and uncertainties with school receded a little but September wasn't far away.

Tryfan Expedition

Lenny started the new school year that September determined to really get to work this time. He had decided to knuckle down and do his best. He started his lessons that September in high spirits. But it wasn't easy, Lenny was up at 5-45am to do his marking up, then when he got home, take care of his little sister Julie and get her to and from nursery. Lenny's mum hadn't been well and had a spell in hospital followed by some convalescents. So it was all a bit of a rush to get to and from school on time.

A new boy joined the school; a larger than life character called Tim Harrison. Lenny and Timmy became instant best friends. Lenny found that they lived quite close together and joined him in the mornings to go to school. Timmy's mum had a Mini Minor and helped Lenny some days by dropping off his sister at Bertie Road Nursery. Timmy's house was in Common Lane and was quite modern. His mum and dad had just had an extension built which made a self contained apartment, with its own side entrance. This was to be known as Tim's Pad. Lenny transferred his snooker table round to Tim's Pad that had its own T.V. and music centre, which made it a really cool place to hang out. Lenny had his first shave there. Timmy's parents hardly ever came in.

It wasn't long before Tim's Pad was being widely talked about and it became a kind of mini youth club with girls being most welcome. Understandably some parents who heard about this were concerned at the lack of supervision. One girl wanted to meet up with Lenny and they arranged to see each other at Tim's Pad. They got together in Timmy's bedroom when suddenly there was a sharp knock on the front door, Timmy went through to answer, and it was none other than the mother of the girl in Timmy's bed, demanding to see her daughter, the girl leapt out fully clothed and departed but in her panic to leave had forgotten her knickers! When the story and knickers hit school it caused major disruption and mayhem to the dismay of Dorothy. The girl's mother went to see Dorothy and the knickers were retrieved from Timmy's pocket. Timmy didn't get into any real trouble as his dad was a member of the golf club.

After dark Lenny and Timmy would go into the Common then climb down onto the railway track which cut straight through into the town with a get off point by Priory Road chippie. Then purchase double portions of chips to eat on their return, diverting up to the rear entrance of the golf club, where the lads syphoned off some sweet cider to quench their thirst. They lay on the floor boards of the haunted house gazing up through the rafters in wonder at the night sky, accompanied by their ghostly chums!

The head girl who was Dorothy's pet was six months older than all the other pupils in the school and was being groomed for stardom to be displayed as a shining example of modernity. As Lenny's secretary she engaged with him but always seemed a bit stand offish and something of a prude. Suddenly she made it clear that she thought she was missing out on all the fun and wanted some action. Lenny and the girl met at Tim's Pad and nature took its course despite the fact that the two young people had never particularly liked each other.

Lenny's enthusiasm for school was rewarded by the great news that two school trips were being planned, one to Lilleshall National Sports Centre where the England team had trained earlier that year then lifted the World Cup, and one to Wales. For the latter trip there was going to be a new camping club run by Mandy and a new teacher called Mr Barthorpe, nick-named Bartholomew. Anyone who wanted to go on a camping trip was free to put down their name. Lenny's good friend Tony Stock, nicknamed 'Brains,' because he knew everything, warned Lenny he better get his name down sometime soon as there was only a limited number of places. As he loved cross-country running and out door pursuits and was already an accomplished mountaineer having conquered Scafell Pike, which is the highest mountain in England, Lenny was quick to get his name on the list.

At the first meeting of the camping club, all the lads that had been accepted were given a list of equipment needed for the forthcoming expedition. They had to supply themselves with a rucksack, anorak, sleeping bag and a proper pair of climbing boots. The school was to supply tents, primus stoves and utensils along with the food. They were told that they would be on an astronauts diet of dried food, all that needed to be added was boiling water. The second meeting of the camping club was a kit check and practice erecting the tents and lighting the primus stoves.

The final meeting of the camping club was all about map and compass-reading. A field exercise had been devised by Mandy. He dropped the lads off at a village named Hunningham, in the car park of The Red Lion pub, with instructions only to use map and compass to find a pub called The Stag, which was in the near by village of Offchurch. The lads were split into three groups and set off, Lenny realised straight away that he knew these lanes like the back of his hand as he had been this way many times on his bike to go fishing at the Grand Union Canal. So his group walked straight through in quick time to the beer garden at the Stag where they refreshed themselves with a bottle of sweet cider from the outdoor. When Mandy turned up some time later he had a good idea what had happened but took it as good spirit. Now the lads had completed their preparation and were ready for the assault on Wales.

Bartholomew was the new games teacher and didn't need reminding that we had just lifted the World Cup. He seemed to like football and Lenny who was used to being in charge of everything football didn't feel put out, the lads thought he was a good guy, if not a little green as he was fresh out of collage. Abbey had finally got a football pitch and were now in a school league and had fixtures to play. The matches were played straight after-school and Lenny remained captain and picked the side.

Lenny's new best mate Timmy was the most unlikely footballer, but Lenny put him straight in the team which raised a few eyebrows from the staff, his strength was his strength, but he could not run, however if he did connect with the ball it could go a very long way. Mandy came along to see what all the fuss was about and Abbey were losing 1-0. Abbey had one of the best goalkeepers in Warwickshire by the name of John Dannerman big strong and very brave. Lenny got caught in possession and passed back to John but put it over his head to score an own goal. Mandy burst out laughing and found it hard to contain himself. Abbey pressed on and Lenny scored a goal at the other end to bring the score to 2-1. Jim Tibbits noted for his bone crunching tackles was taking no prisoners and things looked all over when Timmy struck a lose ball from the centre circle that resulted in a wonder goal and saved the game. Mandy wasn't laughing now.

A few days after the match a complaint landed on Dorothy's desk about Jim Tibbits and his style of tackling, which Lenny fully supported but Dorothy didn't. Lenny's view was what does she know about tackling but the incident resulted in Jim losing his prefects badge and being suspended for one month.

During one match Lenny was hit in the delicates which produced the most unimaginable sick feeling, Lenny was led off into the dressing rooms in a state of delirium. It was explained to Lenny that a cold wet sponge was a good cure but on this occasion there wasn't one available so a cold hand would be just as good. Lenny always thought this to be a strange remedy but never said anything about it and felt quite embarrassed.

The lads had to take care of their football shirts and one was put back damaged. It caused uproar and everybody was in for detention, they were told to confess or name the perpetrator, nobody confessed and nobody was fingered, so Dorothy suspended the football team from the league.

However the expedition to Wales was on and just as good as had been promised. Mandy had obtained a dilapidated old Bedford work bus with side facing bench seats which the boys joked had come from 'Stickly,' the local scrap yard. Despite the exhaust fumes pouring into the back, at least one boy getting sick on the way, and the petrol tank leaking, even getting to

Picture 19: Bedford Work Bus.

Wales was good fun. Lenny and John had secretly brought their fishing tackle and had very ambitious plans to go poaching for trout after dark, when the teachers were asleep. It turned out to be quite cold and they didn't get much sleep with their wet socks. So a good hot meal in the morning would be most welcome, hot it was tasty it was not crunchy mashed potato hard peas and dried biscuits but it was fun.

It would be a day long trek and the boys were told that they were going to climb Tryfan, a well-known mountain in Wales, and quite a demanding hike. They were all fit and more than prepared for it. As they walked up, Lenny and his friend found a camera that had apparently been lost left behind by an earlier hiker. They picked it up and mucked around with it, taking pictures. When they reached the summit, a meander of a river far below could be seen. Lenny was quite pleased with himself for recognising the geographical features that had been talked

Picture 20: Tryfan Meandering View.

about in the geography class with Mr Price. He took a photo of it and of some rock formations with the idea of presenting them back at school. Lenny remembered the fact that nobody had a camera on their trip to London and wasn't going to miss this opportunity to take some snaps and got the whole party together to capture the image. After spending a little time stepping between the two enormous boulders called Adam and Eve it was time to go. Descending from the summit of Tryfan Lenny could not have known at this time but from here on in it would be all down hill.

Picture 21: Tryfan Rock Formations.

Back at the camp the film was used up and they debated what they should do with the camera that had been found. It had been lost, so perhaps it was a case of finder's keepers? Lenny had largely lost interest in it and removed the film. And passed the camera

Picture 22: Tryfan Expedition Party.

to John, when one of the other boys said he wanted to keep it, he shrugged his shoulders and said that that was fine for him.

The lads were tired after a hard day's climb and looked forward to going home in the morning. The expedition was almost complete there was just the challenge of getting back to the Abbey. The lads loaded up the van and when Mandy tried to start it the battery was flat, no problem with a dozen bodies to bump it. After a four hour fume filled journey the lads arrived safely back at the Abbey. The lads felt a great sense of achievement and proud of what they had done, Lenny vowed he would never forget it, but they were all glad to be safely home for a hot meal and some dry socks.

Abbey was in the early stages of planning the other school trip, this time to Lilleshall National Sports Centre where the England football team trained prior to lifting the World Cup. Thunder-Guts told the class that the last school she had worked at visited Lilleshall and the full West Ham team were there including Bobby Moore and Geoff Hurst. They all had their photos taken with the team. There would be professional coaches there and scouts from some of the big clubs. It sounded to Lenny like the chance of a lifetime, which must not to be missed. There would also be hockey and netball for the girls.

Picture 23: Kenilworth Clock.

Disaster

Shortly after the Welsh trip had returned there was a terrible tragedy in Wales when a slag heap covered the mining village of Aberfan, including the local school, killing almost all the children and their teachers. In the aftermath, people all over Britain debated how best they could help the stricken village. In Lenny's school the children were visibly shaken and it was suggested to Lenny that they could have a collection and issue an invitation to the Welsh families to come and visit them in Kenilworth. This idea would be put to the school committee at the next meeting.

However, before Lenny could propose the plan, everything went horribly wrong!

It all started when the father of the boy who had the camera saw the gadget among his son's possessions. Fearing that he had taken something valuable and might get in trouble, the father immediately notified the school. Dorothy personally conducted the initial investigation and was less than satisfied with the outcome. Lenny had been fingered she sensed the boys were holding back some important information which convinced her that the camera had been stolen and was determined to prove it then bring the matter to a speedy conclusion.

Dorothy declared in her dramatic style that she was calling in the police to get to the bottom serious incident! The detectives arrived and set up shop opposite Dorothy's office where

Ma Parker usually took needle work, this was to be their incident room. All the suspects were lined up in the corridor ready to be called for interrogation, the lads didn't feel that concerned as they felt there was a simple explanation and the matter was being blown out of all proportion. Lenny was the last to be called in and gave a simple account and answered all of their questions under caution and was surprised that the film from the camera was never mentioned, which was the whole point as far as Lenny was concerned, but they had missed a vital clue, he thought it best to keep quiet.

The explanation why the camera was not handed to Mandy was a little tricky to explain. It came out as Lenny didn't think it was that important and left it for somebody else which Dorothy found less than convincing. Lenny could hardly say he was protecting the party from the fact that they were all complicit in front of the camera and wanted a few snaps for the geography teacher. The fact that they were all tired cold wet and hungry, yes a possible mistake but surely not a crime! But Dorothy didn't see it that way she could taste blood and was determined to get her man.

The result of the police investigation revealed that Lenny had been the one to find the camera in the first instance, a case of dumb bad luck! Finally the school principal had the excuse she had been looking for to rid herself of this turbulent pest a lad she had never approved of yet was her own creation. She told Lenny that he had to go and that he had brought nothing but shame and disgrace to the school. He was now relived of all his duties, denied privileges, and excluded from taking part in any out of school activities, including the county football trials. He could stay until Easter when he was fifteen and would be old enough to legally depart the education system but that was it. If he behaved his record would read only his grades, if he got into any further trouble he would be expelled which would be recorded in 'red' on his final report!

The camera that had caused all the trouble was returned to its owner, who turned out to be a hiker from Ireland. A thank-you note and a gift of some Irish linen handkerchiefs arrived with the post at Lenny's house, but they were no consolation for the devastation that the incident had caused, but it did finally prove that the lads had not stolen it. Lenny regretted what had happened and the trouble it had caused for Mandy and Bartholomew who had given up their free time for the benefit of the lads, Lenny wished things should be different but discovered the Kenilworth clock marks time which cannot be put back!

But what of the film! Best to talk not!

Sufferance

Stripped of his role as head boy Lenny knew that he was only there on sufferance. He knew that the principal had always disliked him and regretted the fact that he had been elected to a position of responsibility which had led to his downfall. Lenny's parents were disappointed by what had happened, but in those days '*Theirs was not to reason why*,' people rarely disagreed openly with those in authority. It wasn't thought that there were any governors or anything like that just the dictator. There was some talk about the possibility of transferring to the Catholic School of Dormer, even though Lenny had always been to Church of England schools his family ethos was Catholic, Dad had always said don't say anything about it. Lenny was quite interested in the possible change of schools, and after some enquires it became a real possibility. It was kind of put on the back burner to see what would happen but Lenny openly discussed the move to defy his plight.

Meanwhile the reality had sunk in that there would be no more football and no trip to Lilleshall. Lenny had become aware that almost all the staff had sent him to Coventry and would only engage with him on an academic level and there wasn't much of that.

Lenny could not have known but as he entered assembly this day it would be for the last time. Once a week in the school hall there was a service followed by a reading the reading was given by Mr Lewis, nicknamed Bernie. On completion of his reading he would ask a question relating to the reading, and reward a red tally to the person who came up with the correct answer. The lads called this Bernie's question time and found it quite amusing on this day the reading went as follows.

Vincent Paul wasn't a bad sort of a priest and wasn't a good sort of a priest either he was sort of ordinary and on to the conclusion of the reading. Followed by Bernie's question time, this day the question was, 'What kind of a priest was Vincent Paul?' which drew blank looks and a deathly silence from the whole assembly. A few moments passed then Bernie coerced the silent crowd to give him an answer, there started to be some giggling and disturbance coming from the back of the hall where Lenny and Timmy were sat slumped in their chairs. Bernie turned fluorescent and demanded an answer to the question, then to his and everybody's surprise including Timmy, Lenny limply razed his hand, giggling rippled out as they knew they were in for a treat. Fearing the worst Bernie ordered somewhat impolitely Lenny to stand and answer the question, in a muffled voice he replied 'like you lot,' which Bernie didn't hear clearly and requested clarity to which Lenny replied in a firm clear voice, 'ordinary sir.' The whole assembly collapsed in fits of laughter as they thought Lenny had said something untoward as they were all clueless as to the answer. After Bernie had restored calm and control he spluttered out 'correct' there was a stunned silence then Bernie said 'collect a tally from my room after assembly.'

Lenny proudly left assembly and went to wait in the corridor outside Bernie's room where he could see back through, large plate glass windows into the hall where Bernie and Dorothy were in talks, they filed out together.

Dorothy had a style of her own when it came to walking partly influenced by her top heavy anatomy which created a forward leaning stance with her legs doing a sort of goose step to prevent her from toppling over; she peeled off into her office.

The deputy head and principal English teacher of the school was Bernie, who signalled Lenny to enter his room, not sure if deputy was ever aware, but the lads had an unwritten rule never to stand directly in front of him, which resulted in much fidgeting and shuffling of feet. 'Now then Leonard' spluttered out 'I have just been informed that I can't reward you for your performance during assembly this morning, as you are aware you are denied all privileges.' Lenny replied 'that's not fare I was the only one to listen to your sermon,' Bernie said there was nothing he could do about it and that was that. Lenny said that it was a waste of time having assembly which had just been proven because nobody listened to it. Lenny was spoiling for a fight and declared that Bernie's audience of one was now none as Lenny would not be attending any more assembly's, Bernie hit back, that Lenny had to attend or he would be expelled, countered by you must be really desperate to keep your audience of one, and I will not be attending any more. Bernie said that Lenny would have to tell that to head.

Bernie left to explain the situation to Dorothy who thought it needed dealing with straight away so Lenny was summoned to appear. Dorothy declared that if Lenny refused to attend assembly he would be 'expelled' Lenny said 'I refuse to attend on the grounds that my family ethos is Catholic and you can't expel me for that!' They had no idea and it took them completely by surprise, there was a lot of looking at each other then Lenny was dismissed to his form room. Later that day orders came from 'above,' that from now on Lenny was to sit outside the principals office during assembly.

All the children passed by Lenny on their way to assembly and when the forth year came there was a lot of banter and those who didn't know already soon became aware of the rationale for his exclusion.

The only reason left now for Lenny to enter the school hall was to have his dinner. He had always enjoyed the dinners at Abbey that were a cut above his previous schools and there was the social aspect. He was very friendly with a beautiful little girl named Julie Waite from Stoneleigh, her hair was styled in ringlets and she was always chatty, friendly and fun to be with. There was another girl on the same table who was a frumpy monitor, who resented the attention Lenny paid to Julie so she reported Lenny for using bad language which had never worried her in the past before. Dorothy ordered Lenny into her office which was very familiar by now and said that the girl who had complained was so traumatised, that she could not repeat the word but had been brave enough to write it down. Lenny thought what a load of crap! Dorothy pushed a piece of paper under his nose with a word on it and said 'Is this the word you used?' 'Yes' replied Lenny. 'You are now excluded from school dinners and must leave the school premises during lunch time.' Lenny thought that this was a set up for if everybody who used a bad word in the hall was excluded the hall would be half empty.

Timmy was in a different class to Lenny which housed one of the biggest lads in the school. Timmy decided to bring in a water pistol and down by the school gate squirted this big lad on the back of his neck, then promptly hide the weapon. When the lad looked round he could see Lenny laughing and thought that Lenny had squirted him. He was up for a fight, a crowd gather round then he stormed over in full stride slipping off his satchel calling Lenny a dirty catholic. Lenny wasn't bothered about the name calling, but when he stepped into his space in such an aggressive manner, Lenny bopped him on the chin and he went down like a sack of potato's and declined to get up, being catholic was never mentioned again.

Now the general consensus seemed to be that that was it, so far as Lenny's education was concerned. To cap it all, off Lenny's beloved England football shirt had been stolen from his duffle-bag. It was Lenny's most valued possession which could not be overstated. It was simply priceless it was totally unique in its day and could not be purchased. One afternoon Lenny went to his duffle-bag and to his horror found his England football shirt had gone the bag was in the closed position and could not have fallen out. Lenny looked frantically around but it was nowhere to be seen. Lenny went straight to the school office and reported it missing which drew little interest from the secretary who said she would make a note of it and to have a look in lost property.

After a day or two it became apparent that it was of no interest to the staff, and Lenny began to feel he was being treated as a culprit instead of a victim. Maybe he was acting up and being a drama queen. The staff didn't engage with him and he daren't tell his parents after everything else they would go mad. Lenny did everything possible to find his beloved shirt, even 'Brains' enquiries drew a blank, the shirt had vanished and he suffered in silence. Who, could have been behind its disappearance and for what reason? Given the fact that the shirt was so easily recognisable would have made it a bit of a 'Hot-Potato.'

Picture 24: 1 Dorothys Office. 2 School Office. 3 Exit.

Angry and hurt, Lenny started to go off the rails. At lunch times he roamed the streets and when he could, he bought a bottle of cheap cider and used it to take the edge off his formless grief. Lenny was in a really dark place, and counting the days to his departure. He felt very isolated and depressed. With a couple of close friends in his classroom they discussed suicide as being a possible way out but how to do it? Brains thought the best way would be to put your head in the oven and turn the gas on without lighting it then go to sleep. During 1960s when coal gas was still supplied in Kenilworth, it was a very popular choice but the plan for 1970s home's was to convert them to much cleaner burning north sea gas which was none poisonous, so it was thought that method would die out.

Lenny's last day of school dawned and he bowed to the inevitable. During the afternoon he was kept in the art room with Mr Derbyshire, a new teacher of calming influence. Now the scene was set for the final act. At about 2-30pm Mad Ned came in, and said Lenny had to go with him to the school office, Lenny knew what that meant the moment had arrived with his escort to the gallows; no doubt all carefully choreographed by Dorothy.

At the school office the glass window slid aside expectantly, as Lenny was handed a brown envelope with his name on it, followed by the words, 'You can go now,' he placed the envelope in his satchel as the window sliced shut; Lenny turned and pushed open the door to be met by a rush of chilled air as he stepped over the threshold. 'No band playing, No bunting, No goodbye,' Lenny remained composed as the door closed quietly behind him. Hoping against hope to hear a voice say, 'Come back Len, come back,' but it wasn't to be. 'Alone' and for the last time mounting his bike at the school gate, cap pulled over his eyes, tears streaming down his face. It shouldn't have been like this he sobbed. *'Someone had blundered!'*

About the Author

Len was born in Coventry and grew up in Kenilworth, where he has spent the majority of his adult life. Now retired, Len devotes most of his time to caring for his two beautiful children, bringing them to and from school and their many after-school activities. Through them and their joy of learning, he has been able to reassess his own educational experiences.

9 7 8 1 9 0 9 6 4 4 5 7 1

An environmentally friendly book printed and bound in England by www.printondemand-worldwide.com

PEFC Certified

This product is
from sustainably
managed forests
and controlled
sources

www.pefc.org

PEFC/16-33-415

MIX

Paper from
responsible sources

FSC® C004959

This book is made entirely of sustainable materials; FSC paper for the cover and PEFC paper for the text pages.

Reprint of # - C0 - 229/152/9 - PB - Lamination Gloss - Printed on 31-May-17 08:16